THE VEGETARIAN
COOKBOOK FOR KIDS

The vegetarian cookbook for KIDS

EASY, SKILL-BUILDING
RECIPES FOR YOUNG CHEFS

JAMAICA STEVENS

PHOTOGRAPHY BY ELYSA WEITALA

ROCKRIDGE
PRESS

To my mother, who instilled in me a love for
vegetarian cooking and world cuisines as a child.

Interior and Cover Designer: Carlos Esparza
Art Producer: Sue Bischofberger
Editor: Erum Khan
Production Editor: Sigi Nacson
Production Manager: Michael Kay

Photography © 2021 Elysa Weitala; food styling by Victoria Woollard

Author photo courtesy of Robyn Kessler Photography

ISBN: 978-1-64876-938-2
eBook 978-1-64876-270-3
R0

CONTENTS

INTRODUCTION

My love for cooking started when I was a kid. I would experiment in the kitchen, combining all sorts of ingredients to create different flavors. I enjoyed watching cooking shows and cooking with my mother, and I would often try to create my own recipes. Not everything I made came out tasty, and my mother didn't believe in wasting food. So, if I cooked it, I had to eat it. This forced me to learn quickly from my mistakes. I am excited to share with you what I've learned over the years!

I love cooking because it gives me an opportunity to be creative, and I hope that the recipes in this book will encourage you to try new things and be creative, too. I especially love cooking with lots of different kinds of vegetables and fruits. They're colorful, full of flavor, and nutritious.

In this cookbook, we'll learn the basics of vegetarian cooking and cover a wide range of recipes. Even if you aren't vegetarian, you can still enjoy eating plant-based meals! In the first chapter, we'll review cooking basics and kitchen safety. The rest of the chapters will go through everything from breakfast, snacks, lunch, and dinner all the way to dessert. Some of these recipes are very simple, like a creamy smoothie bowl, and others are more advanced, like a savory galette. I encourage you to try making every recipe in the book and to swap out ingredients that you don't like for others that you do. You may find that you're good at coming up with your own recipes, and maybe someday you'll grow up to write a cookbook of your own. You never know!

CHAPTER 1

Let's Cook Vegetarian

In this chapter, we're going to talk about all the things you need to know to be successful in the kitchen. We'll review what vegetarian cooking is, all the delicious ingredients you should keep at home, and how to prepare those ingredients safely. We'll also discuss what tools you need and the basic techniques every beginner chef should know—from measuring and mixing to boiling and safely using the stove. This chapter will get you ready to make every recipe in this book and, by the end of it, I hope you'll be confident and ready to start cooking delicious vegetarian food.

WHAT IS VEGETARIAN COOKING?

Vegetarian cooking simply means cooking without meat, fish, or chicken. Vegetarian cooking uses lots of vegetables and fruits, as well as grains, beans, lentils, nuts, and seeds. Just like any other type of cooking, vegetarian snacks and meals are made using a wide variety of cooking techniques.

Whether you are just starting to explore vegetarian cooking or already have experience, you will find that the recipes in this book are delicious, healthy, and as much fun to prepare as they are to eat! Vegetarian cooking is easy once you understand the basics, which we'll review right now.

BEFORE YOU BEGIN

Whenever you're in the kitchen, it's smart to follow some basic rules. These rules help cooking go more smoothly, and they also make sure you're being as safe as possible.

KNOW WHAT YOU NEED. Always read through the recipe from start to finish so that you know what tools and ingredients you'll need. You don't want to get halfway through a recipe and find that you're missing an important ingredient!

ASK FOR HELP. If you don't know how to do something, or a task seems too hard, ask an adult for help. A lot of the recipes in this book will require some adult help here and there. It's a good idea to read through a recipe with an adult and ask them if they are comfortable with you cooking on your own or if they want to help you.

PREP YOURSELF. Wash your hands before you handle food, and make sure to tie back your hair if it is long. (You don't want to find a hair in your food—that's pretty gross!) If you have an apron, wear one to keep your clothes clean.

PREP YOUR PLACE. Get out the tools and ingredients you need for the recipe before you start cooking. Then measure and cut the ingredients so you are ready to start.

LESSEN THE MESS. Cooking is so much fun, but cleaning up a huge mess isn't. Try to clean up your work space as you go so there's less to do at the end.

STAY SAFE. This is the most important rule of all! It's no fun to get hurt, and there are many things in the kitchen that can be dangerous if you're not careful. When using a knife, the oven, or the stove, make sure to follow the safety suggestions outlined in this chapter.

Stovetop

There are two types of stovetops: gas and electric. A gas stove has a visible flame, but an electric stove has a heating element that may not look hot even when it's on. Both types can get very hot super fast—and stay hot for a while even after they're turned off. It's important to always keep an eye on your food when it's on the stove to make sure it's not burning or boiling over. I suggest starting out using low to medium heat on the stove, and not cooking over high heat until you have a lot of experience. (The exception is when you're boiling water, like for pasta.) When you're finished cooking, make sure to turn off the burner, and don't put anything—not even an empty pot!—on the burner after it's turned off.

Oven

Before you turn on your oven, make sure it's empty. Check where the rack is placed, and move it higher or lower if you need to. Then you can preheat the oven to the temperature called for in the recipe. The oven takes a little bit of time to heat up, and every oven is different—some will beep when they get to the temperature they are set at. The metal racks get very hot, so you'll need to use oven mitts every time you put something in the oven. Once you have put your item in the oven, make sure you set a timer for the amount of time given in the recipe. Try not to open the oven door too often because it lets the hot air inside escape. You can often take a quick peek by turning on the oven light and looking through the glass door. Do check as you get closer to the end of the cook time—this will help you figure out how much longer the food needs to cook or if it will be ready early. Once your food is done, put on your oven mitts again and very carefully remove the pan, then place it on a cooling rack or on the back of the stovetop so you do not accidentally brush up against it while it's hot. Be sure to turn off the oven when you're finished.

Safety First

1. Wash your hands before you start cooking.

2. Never ever try to catch a falling knife.

3. Make sure your cutting board is stable and not on a slippery surface.

4. Use the right knife for the job.

5. Never add water to a pan that contains hot oil.

6. Clean up any spills on the floor right away so you don't slip.

7. Turn pan handles toward the side so they don't stick out and get bumped.

8. Avoid wearing long hair down and loose clothing or dangling jewelry, and remember to roll up your sleeves.

9. Don't use a wet oven mitt—it will not protect your hands from getting burned.

10. Make sure your oven and stovetop are turned off when you're finished cooking.

GET EQUIPPED

There are various kitchen tools you'll need for the recipes in this book, but you will not need all of them for every recipe. These are just some of the tools I find most useful, but each recipe has a list of the specific equipment you will need to make it.

SPATULAS: You'll need a hard one for flipping food in a pan on the stove and a flexible one for scraping food out of a bowl and folding in ingredients.

WOODEN SPOONS: for stirring food in a pan on the stove.

WHISK: for mixing ingredients and beating eggs. If you don't have a whisk, you can use a fork.

KNIVES: the most important tools in any kitchen! There are many kinds, but the ones you'll use most for the recipes in this book are a small paring knife, a larger chopping knife, and a long serrated knife (for slicing bread).

TONGS: for picking up hot objects to remove them from the heat, flip them over, or move them around.

MEASURING CUPS AND SPOONS: to measure out the correct amount of your ingredients.

PEELER: necessary to remove the skin from some fruits (like apples) and vegetables (like potatoes).

GRATER: for cheese and some vegetables, like carrots and zucchini. Graters are very sharp, so make sure you are paying attention and not going too fast when using one or you might cut your fingers.

ZESTER: most often used on the skin of lemons, limes, and oranges but also for things like ginger, garlic, and hard cheeses like Parmesan—or to create small chocolate shavings for a dessert.

SKILLET: can be used on the stovetop or in the oven (as long as the handle isn't plastic).

POTS AND SAUCEPANS (VARIOUS SIZES): used on the stovetop to make dishes like pasta, rice, soups, and sauces.

BAKING PANS (VARIOUS SIZES): used in the oven for baking things like casseroles, mac and cheese, and brownies.

RIMMED BAKING SHEETS (SOMETIMES CALLED SHEET PANS): for everything from baking cookies to roasting veggies. You want the kind that has a rim all the way around so nothing slides off.

COLANDER OR FINE-MESH STRAINER: for draining and rinsing fruits, vegetables, pasta, and canned beans.

ELECTRIC HAND MIXER OR STAND MIXER: for mixing batter quickly and smoothly and for whipping egg whites or cream.

BLENDER OR IMMERSION BLENDER: to make smoothies, soups, sauces, and even batters.

FOOD PROCESSOR: for mixtures that may be too thick for the blender; they can also chop, slice, and shred. Just remember to always be careful with sharp blades.

CUTTING BOARDS: for protecting countertops when chopping, slicing, and dicing ingredients.

BOWLS: best when oversized so that you do not create a mess when mixing.

PARCHMENT PAPER: to line your baking sheets to prevent the food from sticking.

ON-HAND INGREDIENTS

Some ingredients are so useful for vegetarian cooking that you'll want to keep them in your kitchen at all times. Many of these things can be stored in the pantry, whereas others need to be stored in the fridge or freezer.

Pantry

When stocking your pantry for vegetarian cooking, the goal should be to have a variety of dried, canned, and boxed foods that you can pull out anytime, since they don't go bad quickly.

CANNED/DRIED BEANS: great northern or cannellini beans, pinto beans, black beans, kidney beans, lentils, chickpeas

OILS: olive oil, coconut oil, toasted sesame oil, vegetable oil (such as canola or grapeseed)

NUTS AND SEEDS: walnuts, almonds, peanuts, pistachio nuts; sunflower, pumpkin, flax, chia, sesame seeds. If you plan on storing nuts and seeds for more than a few months, it's better to keep them in the fridge or freezer because they can go bad.

GRAINS, RICE, AND PASTA: polenta, quinoa, oats, different types of rice (such as white, basmati, and brown), your favorite pasta shapes

CANNED OR JARRED VEGETABLES: diced tomatoes, olives, roasted bell peppers, artichoke hearts, pickles

BAKING PRODUCTS: unbleached all-purpose flour, light and dark brown sugar and granulated white sugar (and sugar substitutes, such as agave nectar, honey, and pure maple syrup), baking soda, baking powder, vanilla extract, unsweetened cocoa powder, chocolate chips, cornmeal or polenta, oats

SPICES: salt, ground black pepper, garlic powder, chili powder, paprika, ground cumin, ground cinnamon, ground nutmeg, ground coriander, ground turmeric

DRIED HERBS: oregano, parsley, thyme, basil, dill

MISCELLANEOUS ITEMS: vegetable bouillon cubes and boxed broth, soy sauce or coconut aminos, vinegar (such as balsamic vinegar and rice vinegar), coconut milk, dried fruit, nutritional yeast

Countertop

Some fruits and veggies can be kept in a bowl on your countertop until you're ready to use them. If you have leftover cut pieces, wrap them in plastic and put them in the fridge.

FRUITS: bananas, avocados (until they are ripe, then they go in the fridge)

VEGETABLES: tomatoes, garlic, onions, sweet potatoes, potatoes

Fridge and Freezer

These are the ingredients I keep in the fridge and freezer so that I can always be ready to prep a vegetarian meal:

LEAFY GREENS: spinach, kale, Swiss chard, lettuce, arugula

VEGETABLES AND FRUITS: bell peppers, carrots, cauliflower, zucchini, blueberries, strawberries, apples, oranges, lemons, limes

EGGS AND DAIRY: yogurt, milk, various cheeses, butter, cream cheese, sour cream

NUT/SEED BUTTER: almond, peanut, and sunflower seed butters

CONDIMENTS: mustard and mayonnaise

TOFU (EXTRA-FIRM): a source of protein made from soybeans

FROZEN PEAS: as a side dish or an ingredient in dips, sauces, purees, and pesto

FROZEN SPINACH: for your morning eggs, smoothies, soup, or pasta dishes

FROZEN FRUITS: berries, mangoes, peaches, and cherries for smoothies, baking, and on top of hot cereal

Vegetarian or Vegan?

Vegan cooking doesn't use anything that came from an animal. This means that vegans do not eat meat, chicken, or fish, and they also don't eat eggs or dairy products, like milk, ice cream, yogurt, butter, and cheese. They avoid honey, too, since it comes from bees! Vegetarians don't eat meat, chicken, or fish but do eat eggs, dairy products, and honey.

PRO PREP SKILLS

The best way to master your cooking skills is by practicing. The more you practice, the better you'll get, and soon everyone will want to enjoy the food you cooked. Before you start practicing, let's go over some tips for how to read and follow recipes. These prep skills will help you prepare the recipes in this book—and in other cookbooks, too!

Measuring

Always measure your ingredients carefully so your recipe will turn out properly. For measuring dry ingredients (such as flour or rice), use plastic or metal measuring cups that are meant for dry ingredients. For liquids, use a plastic or glass measuring cup meant for liquids, which has a handle and spout for easy pouring. Measuring spoons can be used for both dry and wet ingredients.

DRY INGREDIENTS

When measuring dry ingredients, always level off your measuring spoon or cup by scraping across the top with the back of a butter knife to make sure you are getting the correct amount. When measuring flour, don't scoop your measuring cup into the flour—this packs the flour too tightly in your cup, and you end up with more than you need. It's best to spoon it into the measuring cup and then level it off. (This doesn't apply to other dry ingredients like sugar, rice, or oats.) Many recipes that use brown sugar call for it to be "packed." This means that you should pack the sugar into the measuring cup tightly by pressing it down with your fingers.

When measuring liquids like water, milk, or vegetable broth, use a liquid measuring cup meant for wet ingredients. Put it on a flat counter so that the cup is level and you can get an accurate measurement. It's helpful to crouch down so you can see if the liquid is at the exact measurement line called for.

Some thick, sticky liquids, like honey or molasses, can be measured in a dry measuring cup. Here's a handy trick: Lightly spray your measuring cup with nonstick cooking spray so that your sticky ingredient slides right out into your bowl!

Cutting

I believe that we eat with our eyes first! So, it's fun to try to make your dishes look pretty. One of the ways to do that is by understanding how to chop, dice, slice, and mince your fruits and vegetables. Not only does a proper cut make your food look better, but it also helps everything cook evenly.

Before you cut anything, make sure your cutting board is steady on the counter. To use a knife properly, hold it firmly in your writing hand. Make a claw shape with your other hand so that your fingers are tucked in when holding the food and are not exposed to the blade of the knife.

Most recipes call for ingredients to be cut in a certain manner. These are some of the many ways you can cut:

JULIENNE: Cut lengthwise into thin sticks. If you're cutting a round object like a carrot or cucumber, you'll need to trim the rounded edges first so you have two flat sides, then cut it into strips.

MINCE: Cut as small as you can. Recipes often call for mincing strong-flavored ingredients that you may not want to get too much of in each bite, like garlic, ginger, and onion.

SLICE: Think of a slice of tomato or cheese on a sandwich. A slice can be thin or thick, depending on the ingredient and the recipe.

DICE: Cut something into cubes—like the dice you use in a game!

QUARTER: Cut something into four even pieces.

HALVE: Cut something into two even pieces.

ROUGHLY CHOP: This is an easy, less formal way to cut your vegetables when they don't all need to be the same size but you still want them to be bite-size, as when making soup or salad.

CHIFFONADE: This fancy-looking cut is often used for fresh herbs: Roll a few leaves into a tube and then slice the tube crosswise to create thin ribbons.

Boiling Water

To boil water, simply pour water into a pot so it's about halfway filled, put the pot on the stove, and set it to high heat (this is the one time you want to use high heat as a beginner). You'll know that the water has come to a boil when you see lots of big bubbles breaking all over the surface. Then you can continue with the recipe.

Mixing

Different recipes will ask you to mix ingredients in distinct ways. It's important to follow the steps in the recipe in the right order. That way you know exactly when each ingredient should be mixed in. You also want to make sure to follow any other mixing instructions in the recipe, because it can affect the way a dish turns out. For instance, a recipe might say to mix the ingredients until smooth or until fluffy.

Vegetarian Solutions

If you choose to eat vegetarian all the time, it's important to make sure you are getting enough protein in your diet. Try using chia and pumpkin seeds, nuts, beans and lentils, quinoa, and tofu for sources of protein. Eggs are a great addition to a vegetarian diet because they are nutrient-rich and high in protein, have lots of vitamins, and can be enjoyed in so many different ways. Some vegetables are also high in protein, like peas, spinach, kale, broccoli, and sprouts.

A good rule of thumb is to include a large variety of vegetables and fruits in your diet to make sure you're getting all the vitamins, minerals, and other nutrients your body needs to stay healthy. A fun and easy way to do this is by "eating the rainbow," or trying to eat as many different colors at each meal as you can. Different-colored fruits and vegetables offer different nutrients, so if you eat a colorful diet, you can be confident you're getting everything you need.

There are also what I like to call "meaty" vegetables, like mushrooms and cauliflower. I call them "meaty" because they are filling and can take the place of meat in many recipes. Other foods that are handy to use in vegetarian cooking are those that take on the flavor of the sauce or spices they are cooked in, like beans and tofu.

ABOUT THE RECIPES

This cookbook's recipes are meant to offer lots of options for vegetarian meals that are fun and simple to make while giving you the chance to practice your cooking skills. I want to show you different ways to create flavors, so you'll find recipes for foods found around the world. For example, when you make the Tofu Banh Mi Sandwich (page 81), you'll learn how to quickly pickle your own vegetables. In the Quinoa Veggie Bowl (page 67), you'll whip up a simple sauce. Or, if you want an easy, satisfying meal that you can create with pantry ingredients, you can make a pot of Three-Bean Chili (page 78). If you are not an adventurous eater, that's fine, too. There are also simple recipes for tasty dishes like lasagna, veggie soup, and broccoli mac and cheese.

Labels

The recipes in this cookbook have handy labels so you can easily find what you're looking for:

- **GLUTEN-FREE** recipes that don't have any ingredients that contain gluten.
- **NUT-FREE** recipes that don't have any nuts.
- **ONE-POT** recipes that can be made completely in the same pot or dish, making them easy for cleanup.
- **30-MINUTE** recipes that can be made in 30 minutes or less, from start to finish.
- **5-INGREDIENT** recipes that call for 5 ingredients or fewer (not including water, salt, pepper, and nonstick cooking spray).

Tips

Throughout this book, you'll find handy "Get Creative" tips that allow you to easily change up the recipes. If you want to learn how to become a more creative and flexible chef, this is an important part of each recipe to read! Some tips offer suggestions for substituting ingredients to make a recipe vegan or gluten-free or nut-free. Other tips provide serving ideas and helpful technique hints.

CHAPTER 2

Breakfast and Brunch

BUILD YOUR SKILLS
HOW TO CUT AN AVOCADO

It's not hard to cut up an avocado, but you do have to be very careful with slippery fruit and a sharp knife! First, cut lengthwise into one side of the avocado until your knife hits the pit inside. Rotate the avocado as you continue to cut the whole avocado in half. When you've gotten all the way around, twist the two halves to separate them. The pit will be in one half. You can either remove it with a spoon or carefully stick your knife in it and then pull it out. If you're using all of the avocado (say, for a smoothie), just use a spoon to scoop the flesh into your blender. If you want cubes or slices, make a slit into the flesh without cutting through the skin, then scoop out the pieces with a spoon. Avocado flesh turns brown after it's been exposed to air, so it's best to cut the avocado just before you need to use it. You can also squeeze lemon juice over the cut surface to help keep it from turning brown.

VEGGIE FRITTATA MUFFINS

PREP TIME: 20 minutes **COOK TIME:** 15 minutes **MAKES:** 6 muffins

Ingredients

Nonstick cooking spray

½ small onion, finely chopped

½ medium bell pepper (any color), finely chopped

¾ cup grated or shredded cheese (any kind)

6 cherry tomatoes, halved

4 large eggs

⅓ cup milk

1 teaspoon salt

Equipment

cutting board and knife

measuring cups

measuring spoons

muffin tin

medium bowl

whisk

oven mitt

> A frittata is like an omelet, but it's baked in the oven. It's similar to a quiche, but without a crust. Usually a frittata is made in one big pan, but here we're making frittata muffins!

1. **Turn on the oven and prep your muffin tin.** Preheat the oven to 350°F. Spray 6 cups of a muffin tin with nonstick cooking spray.

2. **Divide the veggies and cheese.** In each sprayed cup of the muffin tin, put 1 tablespoon chopped onion, 1 tablespoon chopped bell pepper, 2 tablespoons cheese, and 2 cherry tomato halves.

3. **Add the eggs.** In a medium bowl, whisk together the eggs, milk, and salt. Pour the mixture into a glass measuring cup with a spout. Pour the mixture over the ingredients in each muffin cup, leaving about ½ inch of space at the top because the muffins will rise as they cook. Carefully stir the egg in each muffin cup so that it mixes with all the ingredients.

4. **Bake and enjoy.** Bake for 15 minutes, or until the eggs have set and look firm in the middle. Pop the frittata muffins out of the tin and serve.

GET CREATIVE: You can add or substitute almost any type of veggie you like in these muffins. Chopped fresh spinach, broccoli, asparagus, and mushrooms all work great. Avoid potatoes, though, unless they are already cooked.

NUT-FREE

GLUTEN-FREE

SAVORY OR SWEET CREPES

PREP TIME: 10 minutes **COOK TIME:** 10 minutes **MAKES:** 8 to 10 crepes

Ingredients

FOR THE CREPES

7 to 8 tablespoons unsalted butter, divided

1 cup plus 2 tablespoons all-purpose flour

1 teaspoon sugar

¼ teaspoon salt

2 large eggs

1¼ cups milk

¼ cup water

FOR A SAVORY FILLING (OPTIONAL)

Scrambled eggs

Chopped spinach

Shredded cheese

Tomato slices

Avocado

FOR A SWEET FILLING (OPTIONAL)

Fresh berries

Sweet Spiced Apples (page 41)

Jelly

Pure maple syrup

Whipped cream

Confectioners' sugar

Crepes are thin French-style pancakes that are served with a tasty filling inside. They can be folded or rolled. Unlike pancakes, crepes don't contain baking powder to make them rise, so they stay very flat.

TO MAKE THE CREPES

1. **Melt the butter.** Melt 5 tablespoons of the butter in a small bowl in the microwave or in a small saucepan on the stovetop, then set aside to cool slightly.

2. **Combine the dry ingredients.** In a large bowl, whisk together the flour, sugar, and salt.

3. **Add the wet ingredients.** Add the eggs, milk, and water and whisk to combine. Once the butter is cool, add that, too. Whisk everything together until the batter is smooth.

4. **Cook the crepes.** Heat 1 teaspoon of the butter in a medium nonstick skillet over medium heat. Fill a ¼-cup measuring cup almost all the way with batter and pour it into the pan. Immediately pick up the pan by the handle and rotate your wrist so the batter spreads out in a large, thin round, then put the pan back down on the burner. Let the crepe cook for about 30 seconds, until the batter looks like it has set, then use a spatula to flip it over. Cook the other side for about 30 seconds, or until the edges have turned golden brown. Transfer the crepe to a plate.

30-MINUTE

NUT-FREE

measuring spoons

measuring cups

small bowl or small saucepan

large bowl

whisk

medium nonstick skillet

spatula

plate

5. **Make the remaining crepes.** Add another teaspoon of the butter to the pan and make another crepe. Repeat until you have used all the batter. As you cook the crepes, stack them all on the plate so the warmest one will keep the stack warm until you're ready to eat them.

TO FILL AND SERVE THE CREPES

6. **Serve and enjoy.** Fill each crepe however you like, and fold or roll them up!

GET CREATIVE: You can fill crepes with just about anything you can think of. The fun part about eating crepes is that everyone can make theirs just how they like it!

WALNUT-APRICOT GRANOLA

PREP TIME: 10 minutes **COOK TIME:** 25 minutes **SERVES:** 6

Ingredients

½ cup coconut oil

½ cup pure maple syrup

3 cups rolled oats

1 cup chopped walnuts

½ teaspoon salt

¼ teaspoon ground nutmeg

½ cup finely chopped dried apricots

½ cup dried cranberries or raisins

Equipment

measuring cups

cutting board and knife

measuring spoons

rimmed baking sheet

parchment paper

small saucepan

large bowl

wooden spoon

spatula

oven mitts

Oats are a super-healthy grain. They're great for baking with and are most commonly enjoyed as a warm breakfast cereal. In this recipe, we'll be making homemade granola that can be eaten as a cold cereal, a quick snack, or a topping for your yogurt.

1. **Turn on the oven and prep your baking sheet.** Preheat the oven to 300°F. Line a rimmed baking sheet with parchment paper.

2. **Melt the coconut oil and maple syrup.** Combine the coconut oil and maple syrup in a small saucepan and cook over low heat just until the coconut oil is dissolved.

3. **Combine the ingredients.** Put the oats in a large bowl and pour in the coconut oil mixture. Add the walnuts, salt, and nutmeg. Stir until everything is combined and the oats are evenly coated.

4. **Bake the granola.** Dump the granola mixture onto the prepared baking sheet. Spread out the mixture with a spatula. Bake for 15 minutes, then remove the baking sheet from the oven. Give the granola a stir, then spread it out again. Put the baking sheet back in the oven for another 10 minutes.

5. **Add the fruit, let cool, and enjoy.** Remove the baking sheet from the oven and add the apricots and cranberries while the granola is still hot, then set it aside to cool completely. (The granola may appear slightly wet when you first take it out of the oven. That's okay, because it will continue to dry as it cools.) If the granola is stuck together, break it up into smaller pieces when you're ready to eat it. Store leftovers in an airtight container at room temperature for up to 2 weeks.

GET CREATIVE: Try adding seeds and other nuts or dried fruit to this recipe. To make this granola into a sweet treat, add chocolate chips once the granola has cooled. To make the recipe gluten-free, use certified gluten-free oats.

POLENTA PORRIDGE WITH MAPLE SYRUP

PREP TIME: 10 minutes **COOK TIME:** 10 minutes **SERVES:** 2

Ingredients

2 cups water

½ cup polenta

¾ cup canned coconut milk

¼ cup pure maple syrup

½ cup sliced strawberries, raspberries, and/or blueberries (optional)

¼ cup dried coconut (optional)

Equipment

measuring cups

medium saucepan

whisk

Polenta is a type of cornmeal, and I ate it a lot when I was a kid. My mother made polenta in all sorts of ways and taught me how to make it, too. In this recipe, we'll use polenta to make a creamy hot cereal!

1. **Start the polenta.** Pour the water into a medium saucepan and bring it to a boil over medium heat. Add the polenta and whisk it well to make sure there are no lumps.

2. **Let it simmer.** Lower the heat so that you see just a few bubbles popping on top. Simmer for 5 to 8 minutes, stirring occasionally.

3. **Make it creamy and sweet.** Remove the pan from the heat and whisk in the coconut milk. (If the mixture is too thick, add 1 to 2 tablespoons warm water.) Pour into bowls, drizzle with the maple syrup, and top with the berries and coconut, if you like. Enjoy while warm.

GET CREATIVE: You can replace the coconut milk with any type of milk—dairy milk, soy milk, almond milk, rice milk, or oat milk.

AVOCADO TOAST WITH POACHED EGGS

PREP TIME: 5 minutes **COOK TIME:** 15 minutes **SERVES:** 4

30-MINUTE

ONE-POT

5-INGREDIENT

NUT-FREE

Ingredients

Nonstick cooking spray

4 tablespoons water, divided

4 large eggs

4 tiny pinches salt

4 tiny pinches ground black pepper (optional)

1 avocado

4 slices bread

Equipment

measuring spoons

muffin tin

slotted spoon

paper towel

cutting board and knife

fork

oven mitts

> Usually eggs are poached in a pot of water on the stove, but poaching them in the oven is much easier. Avocado toast is also very good with scrambled eggs or fried eggs.

1. **Turn on the oven and prep your muffin tin.** Preheat the oven to 350°F. Spray 4 cups of a muffin tin with nonstick cooking spray.

2. **Prep your eggs.** Fill each sprayed cup of the muffin tin with 1 tablespoon water. Carefully crack 1 egg into each cup containing water, trying not to break the yolk. Sprinkle a tiny pinch of salt and pepper (if using) onto each egg.

3. **Bake your eggs.** Bake for 10 to 13 minutes, depending on how runny you like your egg yolk. Remove each poached egg with a slotted spoon and set on a folded paper towel to absorb excess water.

4. **Prep the avocado.** While the eggs are baking, slice the avocado (see page 16).

5. **Make the toast and assemble.** Toast the bread in the toaster or oven and put a slice on each plate. Divide the sliced avocado among the toast slices and gently mash down the avocado with a fork. Add an egg on top of each and serve.

STRAWBERRY-WATERMELON SALAD

PREP TIME: 15 minutes **SERVES:** 6 to 8

Ingredients

4 cups cubed watermelon

1 cup sliced strawberries

½ cup crumbled
feta cheese

½ cup halved pitted
kalamata olives

10 fresh basil leaves,
roughly chopped

10 fresh mint leaves,
roughly chopped

2 tablespoons extra-virgin
olive oil

1 lemon (for zesting)

Equipment

cutting board and knife

measuring cups

measuring spoons

large bowl

zester

This is one of my favorite salads! I love to eat it for breakfast in the summertime. The sweetness of the watermelon and strawberries complements the salty olives and feta cheese. This salad also makes a great side dish or light snack.

1. **Assemble the salad.** Combine the watermelon and strawberries in a serving bowl and top with the feta. Add the olives and chopped basil and mint.

2. **Top the salad.** Drizzle the olive oil over everything. Zest half the peel of the lemon over the top and serve. (You can save the rest of the lemon for another recipe!)

GET CREATIVE: If you do not like the taste of basil or mint leaves, you can leave either of them out. You could also try swapping out one or both for parsley. The same goes for the olives—if you're not a fan, simply leave them out.

30-MINUTE

NUT-FREE

GLUTEN-FREE

SUPER-MOIST BANANA BREAD

PREP TIME: 20 minutes **COOK TIME:** 1 hour **SERVES:** 8 to 12

Ingredients

Nonstick cooking spray

3½ very ripe bananas

8 tablespoons (1 stick) unsalted butter, at room temperature

¾ cup packed dark brown sugar

1 teaspoon vanilla extract

2 large eggs

1¾ cups all-purpose flour

1 teaspoon baking soda

½ teaspoon salt

2 teaspoons ground cinnamon

Equipment

measuring cups

measuring spoons

9 × 5-inch loaf pan

2 small bowls

large fork

large bowl

whisk

toothpick

oven mitts

> This recipe can be used to make either banana bread or muffins. The flavor will be especially sweet if you let your bananas ripen until the skin is dark brown in some spots.

1. **Turn on the oven and prep your baking pan.** Preheat the oven to 350°F. Spray a 9 × 5-inch loaf pan with nonstick cooking spray.

2. **Combine the wet ingredients.** In a small bowl, mash the bananas with a fork. In a large bowl, whisk the butter and brown sugar together until creamy. Then mix in the bananas and vanilla. Add the eggs, one at a time, and mix well.

3. **Combine the dry ingredients.** In a small bowl, whisk together the flour, baking soda, salt, and cinnamon.

4. **Mix together.** Add the dry ingredients to the wet ingredients and mix just until combined. Try not to overmix.

5. **Bake.** Pour the batter into the prepared pan. Bake for about 1 hour, until a toothpick poked in the center of the loaf comes out clean. Let cool slightly before slicing and serving.

GET CREATIVE: To save time, bake 12 muffins in a sprayed muffin tin for about 20 minutes. To make the recipe gluten-free, use gluten-free flour.

FRUIT SMOOTHIE BOWL

PREP TIME: 10 minutes **SERVES:** 1 or 2

Ingredients

1¼ cups frozen mango chunks, divided

½ cup frozen blueberries or frozen mixed berries

½ cup baby spinach

½ cup almond milk

¼ cup fresh blueberries

1 tablespoon sliced almonds

1 tablespoon pumpkin seeds

Equipment

measuring cups

measuring spoons

cutting board and knife

blender

A smoothie bowl is just a really thick smoothie that you eat out of a bowl with a spoon. It's kind of like eating frozen yogurt. Usually smoothie bowls have some kind of topping, like fresh fruit, dried fruit, nuts, or granola. Walnut-Apricot Granola (page 20) would be a great topping!

1. **Prep the topping.** Thinly slice ¼ cup of the frozen mango chunks and set aside for the topping.

2. **Blend it up.** Put the remaining 1 cup frozen mango chunks, frozen blueberries, spinach, and almond milk in a blender, put on the lid, and blend until smooth.

3. **Decorate and enjoy.** Pour the mixture into one or two bowls. Top with the sliced mango, fresh blueberries, almonds, and pumpkin seeds and dig in.

GET CREATIVE: Try adding more toppings and have fun using them to decorate the smoothie bowl. Also, try different combinations of fruit in the blender, like frozen bananas, frozen pineapples, and orange juice.

30-MINUTE

GLUTEN-FREE

CHAPTER 3

Snacks and Small Bites

BUILD YOUR SKILLS

HOW TO ROLL DIFFERENT TYPES OF BALLS

Since we are making veggie balls, cheese balls, and peanut butter brownie balls in this chapter, I thought it would be a good idea to review this skill. Usually, it's easier to start with cold food when working with your hands since the body heat from your hands will naturally warm up the food. When working with sticky things like cream cheese or peanut butter, it's important to form the balls as soon as you take the ingredients out of the fridge. One of my tricks is to lightly coat my hands with cooking oil or cooking spray to help prevent the ingredients from sticking to my hands. The veggie balls are not sticky, so the oil isn't necessary, and rather than use a rolling motion with your hands, you will cup your hands to gently squeeze and pat the balls so the ingredients stick together.

BAKED VEGGIE BALLS

Ingredients

8 tablespoons (1 stick) salted butter

1 (10-ounce) package frozen chopped spinach, thawed

4 large eggs

½ large onion, finely chopped

½ medium carrot, finely chopped

¼ cup finely chopped mushrooms

1½ cups large bread crumbs or stuffing mix

½ cup grated or shredded cheese (any kind)

My sister asks me to make these for every family event—she calls them "little pockets of goodness." They are a cross between a quiche and stuffing rolled up in bite-size balls! These can be enjoyed fresh out of the oven or made ahead of time and reheated.

1. **Melt the butter.** Melt the butter in a small bowl in the microwave or in a small saucepan on the stovetop, then set aside to cool slightly.

2. **Drain the spinach.** Put the thawed spinach in a fine-mesh strainer and press on it to remove the excess water. If you don't have a fine-mesh strainer, you can take small handfuls of spinach and squeeze the water out (over the sink!).

3. **Combine the ingredients.** Crack the eggs into a large bowl and lightly beat them with a large fork. Add the spinach, onion, carrot, mushrooms, bread crumbs or stuffing mix, and cheese. Once the butter is cool, add it to the bowl and mix everything together with the fork. Cover the bowl with plastic wrap and chill in the fridge for at least 1 hour to let the mixture set.

(Continued)

NUT-FREE

BAKED VEGGIE BALLS (CONTINUED)

Equipment

measuring cups

cutting board and knife

small bowl or small saucepan

fine-mesh strainer (optional)

large bowl

large fork

plastic wrap

rimmed baking sheet

parchment paper

oven mitts

4. **Turn on the oven and prep your baking sheet.** Preheat the oven to 350°F. Line a rimmed baking sheet with parchment paper.

5. **Form the balls and bake.** Use your fingers to pull off chunks of the mixture and shape them between your hands into balls about 2 inches across. Place the balls about 1 inch apart on the prepared baking sheet. Bake for 20 minutes, or until the balls look firm.

GET CREATIVE: Try adding any kind of dried or chopped fresh herbs or your favorite spices to this recipe. If you want to make these gluten-free, use gluten-free bread crumbs.

CAPRESE SKEWERS

PREP TIME: 15 minutes **SERVES:** 4

Ingredients

24 cherry tomatoes

12 mini mozzarella cheese balls, drained

12 large fresh basil leaves

1 tablespoon extra-virgin olive oil

1 tablespoon balsamic vinegar

Pinch salt (optional)

Pinch ground black pepper (optional)

¼ lemon (optional)

Equipment

measuring spoons

12 toothpicks

platter

grater or zester (optional)

This recipe is a play on a caprese salad, which is a traditional Italian salad. Many say that its red, white, and green colors represent the Italian flag. This dish has all the same ingredients, but instead of a salad, we'll create a fun, bite-size snack on toothpicks!

1. **Assemble the skewers.** Spear one cherry tomato on a toothpick. Wrap one mozzarella ball with a basil leaf and place it on the toothpick. Add another tomato on the toothpick so that a tomato is on each side of the mozzarella ball. Set the skewer on a platter. Repeat to make all 12 skewers.

2. **Finish and enjoy.** Drizzle the olive oil and balsamic vinegar over the skewers. If you like, sprinkle a pinch of salt and pepper over the skewers. If you have one, use a grater or zester to sprinkle lemon zest over the skewers, if desired. Serve.

GET CREATIVE: When adding salt, pepper, or lemon zest to a dish, always do it from high above the dish so that all of your food is covered. You can add a pitted olive to each skewer or a piece of artichoke heart. If you do not like basil, you can skip it. Try using different colored cherry tomatoes to make the dish more colorful!

5-INGREDIENT

30-MINUTE

NUT-FREE

GLUTEN-FREE

PEA PESTO DIP WITH VEGGIES

PREP TIME: 15 minutes **SERVES:** 8 to 12

Ingredients

2 cups frozen peas, thawed

¼ cup fresh basil leaves

1 teaspoon salt

½ teaspoon paprika (optional)

½ cup extra-virgin olive oil

½ cup grated Parmesan cheese

½ lemon

Fresh veggies (such as carrot sticks, cherry tomatoes, cucumber slices, cauliflower florets, and snap peas), for serving

Equipment

measuring cups

measuring spoons

food processor or blender

zester

In this recipe, we'll learn how emulsion works. Emulsion is a way to mix two things that normally don't mix well together. (You'll have another chance to practice this in the Pesto Pasta on page 68.) This process is often used when making salad dressings, sauces, and dips.

1. **Make the pesto.** Combine the peas, basil, salt, and paprika (if using) in a food processor or blender, put the lid on, and blend until smooth and creamy. To emulsify, while the machine is running, slowly pour in the olive oil through the opening at the top and blend until smooth. Add the Parmesan and blend until combined.

2. **Enjoy with veggies.** Transfer the pesto to a serving bowl and zest the lemon half on top. Serve as a dip with your favorite fresh veggies.

GET CREATIVE: Mint also goes well with peas, so you can try replacing the basil with mint or add mint along with the basil. This dip also works well as a sandwich spread and is tasty on crackers.

30-MINUTE

NUT-FREE

GLUTEN-FREE

FRUIT AND NUT
CHEESE BALLS WITH CRACKERS

PREP TIME: 15 minutes **SERVES:** 8

Ingredients

2 tablespoons finely chopped pecans

2 tablespoons finely chopped pistachios

¼ cup chopped dried cranberries

2 tablespoons chopped fresh parsley

1 (8-ounce) package cold cream cheese

Crackers or sliced baguette, for serving

Equipment

cutting board and knife

measuring spoons

measuring cups

small bowl

This is the perfect snack to serve to friends, and it also makes a great appetizer for a party or gathering.

1. **Prep the ingredients.** Combine the pecans, pistachios, cranberries, and parsley in a small bowl.

2. **Form the cheese balls.** Cut the block of cream cheese into 2 or 4 equal pieces, depending on the size of cheese balls you want to create. Create a ball with each piece, rolling it between your hands (to reduce the mess, make sure the cream cheese is very cold).

3. **Coat the cheese balls.** Gently toss each ball into the bowl of nuts, cranberries, and parsley, lightly patting the ball to cover the entire outside with the mixture.

4. **Enjoy as a lovely snack.** Serve the cheese balls with crackers or a sliced baguette.

GET CREATIVE: You can swap out the pecans and pistachios for other nuts, such as walnuts or almonds. Or, to make this recipe nut-free, simply replace the nuts with other dried fruits, such as apricots, cherries, or blueberries. To make this snack gluten-free, serve it with gluten-free crackers or bread.

CLASSIC CORNBREAD

PREP TIME: 15 minutes **COOK TIME:** 30 minutes **SERVES:** 9

Ingredients

Nonstick cooking spray

5 tablespoons unsalted butter, at room temperature

3 tablespoons light brown sugar or honey

2 large eggs

1 cup milk

1 cup cornmeal

1 cup all-purpose flour

2 teaspoons baking powder

1 teaspoon salt

Equipment

measuring spoons

measuring cups

8-inch square baking pan

2 large bowls

whisk or spoon

toothpick

oven mitts

This is the cornbread my mother made for us all the time when I was growing up. I love to eat it warm out of the oven with butter and honey. It also goes great with my Three-Bean Chili (page 78).

1. **Turn on the oven and prep your baking pan.** Preheat the oven to 350°F. Spray an 8-inch square baking pan with nonstick cooking spray.

2. **Mix the brown sugar and wet ingredients.** Combine the butter and brown sugar or honey in a large bowl and mix well. Add the eggs, one at a time, and then the milk.

3. **Mix the dry ingredients.** In another large bowl, whisk together the cornmeal, flour, baking powder, and salt.

4. **Combine the wet and dry ingredients.** Pour the dry ingredients into the wet ingredients and mix until smooth.

5. **Bake and let cool.** Pour the batter into the prepared baking pan and bake for 30 minutes, or until a toothpick poked in the center of the cornbread comes out clean. Let cool slightly before slicing and serving.

GET CREATIVE: Try adding ½ cup frozen corn to the batter for added texture! For corn muffins, spray a muffin tin and bake for 17 to 20 minutes.

MANGO-AVOCADO SALSA WITH TORTILLA CHIPS

PREP TIME: 30 minutes **SERVES:** 4 to 6

Ingredients

1 mango

2 avocados

½ lime

3 tablespoons roughly chopped fresh cilantro leaves

½ teaspoon salt

½ teaspoon garlic powder

½ teaspoon paprika

Tortilla chips, for serving

Equipment

measuring spoons

cutting board and knife

spoon

large bowl

GET CREATIVE: If you like spicy foods, you can add chili powder, red pepper flakes, or even hot sauce to this salsa. To make the recipe gluten-free, use 100% corn tortilla chips.

This is one of my favorite salsas. It makes a yummy light snack when served with tortilla chips for dipping. Its fresh, bright flavors also make it easy to pair with lots of different dishes, including Masa Corn Cakes (page 53), Enchilada Casserole (page 83), and Ultimate Veggie Burger (page 88).

1. **Prep the mango and avocados.** Cut a slice off the mango down one side, as close to the pit as you can. Do the same thing on the other side. Cut the flesh into small cubes without cutting through the skin, then scoop out the cubes with a spoon or your fingers. If you can, cut some cubes from the fruit that's still attached to each side of the pit. Put the mango cubes in a large bowl. Cut the avocados into small cubes according to the instructions on page 16. Put the avocado cubes in the same bowl with the mango.

2. **Combine the flavors.** Squeeze the lime half over the mango and avocado to add flavor and to help prevent the avocado from turning brown. Add the cilantro, salt, garlic powder, and paprika and gently stir. Serve with tortilla chips.

30-MINUTE

NUT-FREE

NO-BAKE PEANUT BUTTER BROWNIE BALLS

PREP TIME: 1½ hours (includes chilling time) **MAKES:** 14 to 20 balls

Ingredients

1 (15-ounce) can black beans

½ cup smooth peanut butter

⅓ cup cocoa powder

½ cup rolled oats

3 tablespoons agave nectar or pure maple syrup

3 dates, pitted

Equipment

measuring cups

measuring spoons

strainer or colander

food processor or blender

large bowl

plastic wrap

I know brownie balls made out of black beans may sound strange, but before you say "Yuck," give these a try! You'll be pleasantly surprised. These little balls taste like chocolate fudge—and they're actually good for you!

1. **Drain the beans.** Drain the beans in a colander and rinse under cool running water.

2. **Combine the ingredients.** Put the beans, peanut butter, cocoa powder, oats, agave or maple syrup, and dates in a food processor or blender. (A food processor works better, if you have one.) Blend until the ingredients come together and look like cookie dough. If the dough is too thick for your food processor or blender, try adding 1 to 2 tablespoons water.

3. **Chill the dough.** Transfer the dough to a large bowl, cover with plastic wrap, and put in the fridge for at least 1 hour to let it set.

4. **Create the balls.** Roll the dough into bite-size balls and enjoy! Store leftovers in a covered container in the fridge for 5 to 7 days.

GET CREATIVE: Try rolling the brownie balls in chopped nuts or dried coconut. Or add ½ cup mini chocolate chips to the dough. To make the recipe gluten-free, use certified gluten-free oats.

SWEET SPICED APPLES

PREP TIME: 15 minutes **COOK TIME:** 20 minutes **SERVES:** 12

Ingredients

5 large apples

½ cup water, plus more as needed

1 tablespoon dark brown sugar or pure maple syrup

1 tablespoon ground cinnamon

½ teaspoon ground nutmeg

Equipment

measuring cups

measuring spoons

peeler

apple corer (optional)

cutting board and knife

large pot

wooden spoon

This sweet, chunky applesauce will remind you of an apple pie! In this recipe, we'll learn how to reduce a liquid. The longer you cook the apples with the lid off, the more water will evaporate; this helps concentrate the flavors.

1. **Prep the apples.** Peel the apples. Cut each apple in half, then in half again to make quarters. Cut out the core, then cut each piece in half again. (If you have an apple corer, use that before cutting the slices!)

2. **Combine the flavors.** Put the apple pieces and water in a large pot. Add the brown sugar or maple syrup, cinnamon, and nutmeg and stir with a wooden spoon.

3. **Cook the apples.** Cover the pot and cook over medium heat until the apples start to release their juices, about 10 minutes.

4. **Reduce the liquid.** Uncover the pot and continue cooking to let the water evaporate and soften the apples, about 10 more minutes. If at any point the water in the pot completely disappears and the apples start to stick to the bottom, add 1 to 2 tablespoons more water.

5. **Remove from the heat and let cool.** Enjoy the apples warm or cold. Store any leftovers in an airtight container in the fridge for 5 to 7 days.

GET CREATIVE: These apples make a great filling for Savory or Sweet Crepes (page 18).

CHAPTER 4

Lunches and Small Meals

RAINBOW CORN SALAD

PREP TIME: 20 minutes **COOK TIME:** 10 minutes **SERVES:** 4 to 6

30-MINUTE ONE-POT NUT-FREE GLUTEN-FREE

Ingredients

3 ears corn

1 (15-ounce) can black beans

1 tablespoon vegetable oil

1 small red onion, finely chopped

1 teaspoon salt

½ teaspoon paprika

1 medium orange or red bell pepper, chopped

½ cup halved cherry tomatoes

¼ cup fresh cilantro leaves

1 lime

Equipment

measuring spoons

measuring cups

cutting board and knife

shallow dish

strainer or colander

large skillet

wooden spoon

This colorful salad is best with corn cut fresh off the cobs, but if corn is out of season, you can use 1½ cups frozen corn, thawed.

1. **Prep the corn and beans.** Peel off the husks from the ears of corn and remove the silky strands. Stand one ear of corn in a shallow dish. Carefully slice down each side of the cob so the corn kernels fall into the dish. Repeat with the other two ears of corn. Drain the beans in a colander and rinse under cool running water.

2. **Cook the onion, corn, and beans.** In a large skillet, heat the vegetable oil over low heat. Add the onion, salt, and paprika and cook, stirring occasionally, for 3 minutes. Add the corn and cook, stirring, for another 3 to 4 minutes. Stir in the beans and remove the skillet from the heat.

3. **Add the remaining ingredients and serve.** Add the bell pepper, cherry tomatoes, and cilantro. Cut the lime in half and squeeze both halves over the salad. Stir well and serve warm, at room temperature, or chilled.

GET CREATIVE: This corn salad also makes a great dip for tortilla chips, or it can be used as a filling in tacos, enchiladas, or quesadillas. Just add shredded cheese!

SAVORY HAND PIES

PREP TIME: 30 minutes **COOK TIME:** 20 minutes **SERVES:** 4 to 6

Ingredients

1 (10-ounce) package frozen chopped spinach, thawed

1 garlic clove, minced

2 cups crumbled feta cheese

½ teaspoon salt

¼ teaspoon ground black pepper

2 large eggs

All-purpose flour, for dusting

2 refrigerated pie crusts

A hand pie is just what it sounds like: a little pie you can eat with your hands! A hand pie often looks like a Pop-Tart or empanada, depending on what size and shape you make it.

1. **Turn on the oven and prep your baking sheet.** Preheat the oven to 350°F. Line a rimmed baking sheet with parchment paper.

2. **Make the filling.** Put the thawed spinach in a fine-mesh strainer and press on it to remove excess water. If you don't have a fine-mesh strainer, you can take small handfuls of spinach and squeeze the water out (over the sink!). Put the spinach in a large bowl and add the garlic, feta, salt, and pepper. Mix well.

3. **Make an egg wash.** Crack the eggs into a small bowl and lightly whisk them; set aside.

4. **Prep the crust.** Scatter flour all over a clean work surface to prevent sticking. Put one pie crust on the flour and lightly roll it out with a rolling pin, about ⅛ inch thick. Use a large cookie cutter or a yogurt lid dipped in flour to cut out 5 or 6 rounds. Repeat with the other pie crust.

(Continued)

NUT-FREE

SAVORY HAND PIES (CONTINUED)

Equipment

cutting board and knife

measuring cups

measuring spoons

rimmed baking sheet

parchment paper

fine-mesh strainer

large bowl

large spoon

small bowl

whisk

rolling pin

cookie cutter or yogurt lid

spoon

fork

pastry brush or spatula

oven mitts

5. **Assemble the hand pies.** Put 1 to 2 heaping tablespoons of the spinach-feta mixture in the center of a dough round. Use the back of a spoon to paint the edges of the dough with the egg wash. Fold the round in half over the filling to create a half-moon, and use the tines of a fork to seal the edges together. (If it is sticking, dip the fork in the flour.) Put the hand pie on the prepared baking sheet. Repeat to make all the hand pies. Poke a few holes in the center of each hand pie with a fork. Brush the tops with more of the egg wash using a pastry brush or spatula.

6. **Bake and let cool.** Bake for about 20 minutes, until the crust turns golden. Let cool slightly before serving.

GET CREATIVE: You can use any kind of cheese you like in these hand pies, and you can also add any type of roasted vegetable to the spinach mixture.

CREAMY CAULIFLOWER SOUP AND GRILLED CHEESE

PREP TIME: 20 minutes **COOK TIME:** 1 hour **SERVES:** 4

Ingredients

FOR THE SOUP

1 head cauliflower

1 cup vegetable broth, plus more as needed

½ cup almond milk, plus more as needed

1 garlic clove, lightly smashed

1 teaspoon salt

½ teaspoon ground nutmeg

FOR THE GRILLED CHEESE SANDWICHES

2 tablespoons mayonnaise or unsalted butter

4 slices bread

⅔ cup shredded cheese (any kind you like)

I think of cauliflower as a rock star vegetable because it can be enjoyed in so many different ways: roasted, steamed, as rice, and even raw. When blended it has a creamy texture, so it can also be a substitute for or addition to mashed potatoes. In this recipe, we'll make a wonderfully creamy soup and pair it with a classic grilled cheese sandwich.

TO MAKE THE SOUP

1. **Prep the ingredients for the soup.** Cut the entire cauliflower head (including the stem and any leaves) into 4 to 6 large pieces. Put the cauliflower in a large pot. Add the vegetable broth, almond milk, and garlic clove.

2. **Cook the cauliflower.** Cover the pot and cook the soup over low heat for 30 to 45 minutes, until the cauliflower looks like it is falling apart and is very soft when you poke it with a fork. Remove the pot from the heat, uncover it, and let cool for about 10 minutes.

3. **Make it creamy.** Carefully pour the contents of the pot into a blender. Add the salt and nutmeg. Remove the center cap from the blender lid. Holding a dish towel firmly over the hole to allow the steam to escape,

(Continued)

Equipment

measuring cups

measuring spoons

cutting board and knife

large pot

fork

blender

dish towel

large skillet

spatula

blend until the mixture is smooth and creamy. Add a little more almond milk or broth if the mixture is too thick for the blender. Return the soup to the same pot and keep warm over low heat while you make the grilled cheese.

TO MAKE THE GRILLED CHEESE SANDWICHES

4. **Make the grilled cheese sandwiches.** Spread the mayo or butter on one side of each slice of bread. Heat a large skillet over medium heat. Place 2 slices of bread, mayo side down, in the pan. Divide the shredded cheese on top, then place the other slices of bread on the cheese, mayo side up. Cook until golden brown on the bottom, 3 to 5 minutes. Use a spatula to flip over the sandwiches and then cook the other side for 3 to 5 minutes. Remove the sandwiches from the pan and cut in half.

TO SERVE

5. Serve a half sandwich with each bowl of soup.

GET CREATIVE: This can become a vegan sandwich by simply swapping out the cheese for a vegan cheese and using olive oil instead of mayonnaise or butter.

LEFTOVERS PASTA SALAD

PREP TIME: 15 minutes **COOK TIME:** 15 minutes **SERVES:** 4 to 6

Ingredients

4 teaspoons salt, divided

2 cups small pasta (such as penne or elbow macaroni)

1 cup baby spinach, roughly chopped

1 medium bell pepper (any color), chopped

1 medium tomato, diced

½ cup crumbled feta cheese

⅓ cup sliced pitted black olives

⅓ cup extra-virgin olive oil

1 lemon

1 tablespoon za'atar

Equipment

measuring spoons

measuring cups

cutting board and knife

large pot

colander or strainer

wooden spoon

I call this "Leftovers Pasta Salad" because it's a great use for any extra vegetables you have on hand. If you have leftover cooked broccoli, zucchini, eggplant, asparagus, Brussels sprouts, cauliflower, or even carrots, chop them up and throw them into this salad. It's easiest to dice and chop all the veggies while your water is boiling. In this recipe, we'll use za'atar, a blend of dried herbs and spices often found in Middle Eastern cooking. It's a great addition to salads, flatbreads, and dips. Try adding it to the Caprese Skewers (page 33), Panzanella Salad (page 52), or Easy Flatbread Pizza (page 70).

1. **Make the pasta.** Fill a large pot halfway with water and add 2 teaspoons of the salt. Bring to a boil over high heat. Add the pasta and cook until tender, 8 to 12 minutes. Carefully drain the pasta in a colander, then return the drained pasta to the empty pot.

2. **Mix it all together.** Add the spinach, bell pepper, tomato, feta, olives, and olive oil to the pot. Cut the lemon in half and squeeze the juice on top. Add the remaining 2 teaspoons salt and the za'atar. Mix everything together well and serve warm, at room temperature, or cold.

GET CREATIVE: Leave out the feta cheese if you want to make this a vegan dish.

LENTIL SOUP

PREP TIME: 15 minutes **COOK TIME:** 15 minutes **SERVES:** 2 to 3

Ingredients

1 cup split red lentils

1 tablespoon coconut oil or ghee

1 teaspoon ground cumin

1 teaspoon ground coriander

½ teaspoon ground turmeric

½ teaspoon chili powder

1 garlic clove, minced

2½ cups water

½ cup canned coconut milk

½ teaspoon salt

Naan, lavash, or pita bread, for serving (optional)

Equipment

measuring cups

measuring spoons

cutting board and knife

colander or strainer

medium saucepan

wooden spoon

In this recipe, we'll practice something called *tadka*. This is a method used in Indian cooking in which spices are heated in an oil before the other ingredients are added.

1. **Prep the lentils.** Put the lentils in a colander and rinse under cool running water.

2. **Practice tadka.** In a medium saucepan, heat the coconut oil or ghee over low heat. Add the cumin, coriander, turmeric, chili powder, and minced garlic. Stir very briefly, just until you can smell the spices filling the air.

3. **Cook the soup.** Add the lentils and water and increase the heat to medium to bring the water to a boil. Add the coconut milk and salt. Stir, then reduce the heat to low. Cover the pot and simmer for 15 minutes.

4. **Remove from the heat and enjoy.** Serve the soup warm, with bread on the side, if you like.

GET CREATIVE: Try squeezing a wedge of lime over your bowl of soup and adding some fresh cilantro. You can also add a tablespoon of nut butter to the soup while it's cooking for added flavor and protein.

ROASTED VEGETABLE SANDWICH

PREP TIME: 25 minutes **COOK TIME:** 25 minutes **SERVES:** 4

Ingredients

1 zucchini

1 eggplant

1 red bell pepper

1 red onion

2 garlic cloves

6 tablespoons extra-virgin olive oil, divided

2 teaspoons salt

4 large square pieces ciabatta bread, cut in half

4 ounces feta or mozzarella cheese, sliced

Equipment

measuring spoons

cutting board and knife

large bowl

wooden spoon

2 rimmed baking sheets

spatula

oven mitts

> Roasted vegetables are always good to have in the fridge. You can add them to salads, egg dishes, and pasta or rice dishes, or create this super-yummy sandwich.

1. **Turn on the oven.** Preheat the oven to 425°F.

2. **Cut up your veggies.** Cut long, thin slices of the zucchini, eggplant, bell pepper, and onion. Mince the garlic.

3. **Roast the vegetables.** Put all the veggies in a large bowl and toss with 4 tablespoons of the olive oil and the salt. Divide the vegetables between 2 rimmed baking sheets and spread them out in a single layer. Roast for 20 to 25 minutes, until they are tender and starting to turn brown in spots.

4. **Assemble the sandwiches.** Toast the bread in a toaster or the oven. Drizzle the remaining 2 tablespoons olive oil on 4 pieces of toast, layer some vegetables on top, and add some cheese. Close up the sandwiches with the remaining 4 pieces of toast and enjoy while warm.

GET CREATIVE: You can add a spread (such as the pesto on page 68) or a store-bought olive tapenade to this sandwich. Feel free to roast any other veggies you like, such as sweet potatoes or mushrooms.

PANZANELLA SALAD

PREP TIME: 20 minutes **SERVES:** 4 to 6

Ingredients

1 baguette or loaf of sourdough, ciabatta, or rustic Italian bread

10 fresh basil leaves

1 lemon

¼ cup extra-virgin olive oil

2 tablespoons white balsamic vinegar

½ teaspoon salt

2 shallots, thinly sliced

1 cup thinly sliced English or Persian cucumber

2 cups halved cherry tomatoes

Equipment

measuring cups

measuring spoons

cutting board and knife

small jar (or small bowl and whisk)

large bowl

Panzanella salad is a bread salad! It's normally made of stale bread or a really crusty bread that softens from the juices of the tomatoes, vinegar, olive oil, and lemon juice in the salad.

1. **Prep the bread.** Make large bread crumbs by tearing the bread into bite-size pieces. You will need 2 cups.

2. **Prep the basil.** Chiffonade the basil by stacking several leaves, rolling them up, and then thinly slicing them into ribbons.

3. **Make the dressing.** Cut the lemon in half and squeeze the juice into a small jar. Add the olive oil, vinegar, and salt. Cover and shake well. (If you don't have a jar, you can whisk the ingredients in a small bowl.)

4. **Combine all the flavors.** Combine the shallots, basil, cucumber, tomatoes, and bread crumbs in a large bowl. Add the dressing and toss to coat. Let the salad sit for 10 to 30 minutes, depending on how soft or crunchy you like your bread. The longer you let it sit, the softer the bread will get.

GET CREATIVE: I like adding cubes of fresh mozzarella to this salad. Pitted olives and sliced bell peppers also make great additions.

MASA CORN CAKES (SOPES)

PREP TIME: 30 minutes **COOK TIME:** 30 minutes **SERVES:** 4

Ingredients

2 cups masa harina

1 cup water

½ cup vegetable oil

1 (15-ounce) can refried beans

½ cup shredded cheese (any kind)

1 large avocado

½ cup thinly sliced iceberg lettuce

½ cup diced tomato

1 lime, quartered

Equipment

measuring cups

cutting board and knife

large bowl

wooden spoon

measuring spoons

large skillet

spatula

rimmed baking sheet

oven mitts

Sopes are Mexican corn patties that are often topped with the same types of ingredients you will find in a taco. They are made with masa harina, a type of flour made from ground corn. Masa is also used to make corn tortillas and tamales, and you can easily find it in most grocery stores.

1. **Turn on the oven.** Preheat the oven to 250°F.

2. **Make the corn cakes.** Combine the masa and water in a large bowl and stir until you have a smooth dough. Scoop out 3 tablespoons of the dough and use your hands to flatten it into a round, flat cake. Repeat to use up all the dough.

3. **Cook the corn cakes.** Heat the oil in a large skillet over low heat. When the oil is hot, add the corn cakes and cook for 3 to 4 minutes, until golden brown on the bottom. Use a spatula to flip the corn cakes and cook the other side for 3 to 4 minutes. Set each cake on a rimmed baking sheet as it is finished. (If necessary, cook the corn cakes in batches so you don't crowd the skillet.)

4. **Assemble the corn cakes.** Top each corn cake with some refried beans and cheese. Put the baking sheet in the oven and bake just until the cheese is melted, about 10 minutes.

(Continued)

MASA CORN CAKES (SOPES) (CONTINUED)

5. **Prep the avocado.** While the sopes are in the oven, cut the avocado into cubes according to the instructions on page 16.

6. **Finish the sopes and enjoy.** Top the sopes with the lettuce, tomato, and avocado. Serve with a lime wedge so that each person can squeeze lime on top just before enjoying.

GET CREATIVE: I recommend adding extra toppings like sour cream, fresh cilantro, and salsa or hot sauce if you like things spicy.

SUSHI ROLLS

PREP TIME: 30 minutes **COOK TIME:** 15 minutes **SERVES:** 2

Ingredients

2 cups water

1 cup white rice

2 tablespoons rice vinegar

½ cucumber

½ carrot

2 scallions (white and light green parts)

1 avocado

2 sheets nori

2 tablespoons coconut aminos or soy sauce, for serving (optional)

Pickled ginger, for serving (optional)

> Sushi is a traditional Japanese dish usually made with rice, raw fish, and vegetables. For vegetarian sushi, we simply leave out the fish!

1. **Make the rice.** Pour the water into a medium saucepan and bring to a boil over medium-high heat. Add the rice, and stir until the water is boiling again. Reduce the heat to low, cover the pot, and cook for 8 to 12 minutes, until the rice is tender and all the water has been absorbed. Gently mix the rice vinegar into the cooked rice while it is still warm.

2. **Prep the sushi filling.** While the rice is cooking, cut the cucumber and carrot into thin matchsticks (julienne). Cut the scallions into pieces about the same length as the julienne. Cut the avocado into slices according to the instructions on page 16.

3. **Prep the seaweed paper.** Place one sheet of nori on a bamboo rolling mat or on a dish towel covered with plastic wrap.

4. **Assemble the sushi rolls.** Press half of the rice onto two-thirds of the nori sheet closest to you. Then layer on half of the avocado, cucumber, carrot, and scallions over the rice. Roll the nori away from your body, applying some pressure to create the sushi roll. Remove the sushi roll and put it on a cutting board. Carefully slice the roll in half, then slice each half into

NUT-FREE

GLUTEN-FREE

(Continued)

SUSHI ROLLS (CONTINUED)

Equipment

measuring cups

measuring spoons

medium saucepan

wooden spoon

cutting board and knife

bamboo rolling mat
(or dish towel and
plastic wrap)

3 even pieces, so you end up with 6 pieces. Repeat with the remaining nori sheet, rice, and vegetables to make another 6 pieces.

5. **Serve the sushi rolls.** Serve with coconut aminos or soy sauce and pickled ginger, if you like.

GET CREATIVE: You can create sushi rolls with tofu and your favorite cooked veggies. Some people even like to put cream cheese in their sushi rolls.

ZUCCHINI TART

PREP TIME: 30 minutes **COOK TIME:** 50 minutes **SERVES:** 8

Ingredients

Nonstick cooking spray

2 zucchini

1 tablespoon extra-virgin olive oil

½ teaspoon salt

8 ounces ricotta cheese or goat cheese, at room temperature

1 shallot, minced

1 garlic clove, minced

All-purpose flour, for dusting

1 refrigerated pie crust

Equipment

tart pan (or rimmed baking sheet)

measuring spoons

cutting board and knife

2 medium bowls

wooden spoon

rolling pin

spatula

oven mitts

> A tart can be savory or sweet and usually has a filling in a pie-like crust.

1. **Turn on the oven and prep your baking pan.** Preheat the oven to 375°F. Spray a tart pan or rimmed baking sheet with nonstick cooking spray.

2. **Prep the filling.** Slice the zucchini as thin as you can and put the slices in a medium bowl. Add the olive oil and salt and toss to coat. In another medium bowl, mix the cheese, shallot, and garlic.

3. **Prep the pie crust.** Scatter flour all over a clean work surface to prevent sticking. Put the pie crust on the flour and lightly roll it out with a rolling pin to a 9- or 10-inch round. Transfer the dough to the prepared tart pan or baking sheet. If using a tart pan, press the dough into the bottom and up the sides. If using a baking sheet, roll up the edges of the dough to create a ½-inch border all the way around.

NUT-FREE

(Continued)

ZUCCHINI TART (CONTINUED)

4. **Assemble your tart.** Gently spread the cheese mixture all over the crust. Arrange the zucchini slices in a ring on the outer edge of the crust, with the slices slightly overlapping. Repeat, making a smaller round, and continue working your way into the center until the entire tart is covered with zucchini slices.

5. **Bake and let cool.** Bake for 50 minutes, or until the edges of the crust turn golden. Let the tart cool a bit, then slice and serve warm or at room temperature.

GET CREATIVE: To make your pie crust from scratch, use the recipe for Savory Galette (page 85).

BUILD YOUR SKILLS
HOW TO ROAST VEGETABLES

When roasting vegetables, it's important to cut everything into equal-size pieces so that they cook evenly. Make sure all the vegetables are covered with a light coating of oil and salt before roasting. Spread out the vegetables on a rimmed baking sheet. If the pieces are too close together or stacked on top of each other, they will steam instead of roast. Roast at high heat, and adjust the time depending on what you're roasting. Zucchini, bell peppers, and broccoli take 10 to 15 minutes. Cauliflower, butternut squash, and Brussels sprouts take 20 to 25 minutes. Beets, carrots, sweet potatoes, and potatoes take 30 to 40 minutes. If you're roasting different types of vegetables together, chop heavier, denser vegetables (like sweet potatoes and carrots) into smaller pieces because they take longer to cook than lighter vegetables (like broccoli and bell peppers).

BUTTERNUT SQUASH LASAGNA

PREP TIME: 30 minutes **COOK TIME:** 45 minutes **SERVES:** 10 to 12

Ingredients

Nonstick cooking spray

4 cups butternut squash chunks (from 2 squash)

2 tablespoons extra-virgin olive oil

1 large egg

1½ cups ricotta cheese

½ cup grated Parmesan cheese

¾ cup thinly sliced scallions (white and light green parts), divided

2 (15-ounce) cans diced tomatoes

9 to 12 no-cook lasagna noodles

3 cups grated mozzarella cheese, divided

Lasagna is one of those foods that most people love. What's not to love about layered noodles, cheese, and vegetables? This recipe features butternut squash, but you can replace that with another roasted vegetable of your choice. If you do use butternut squash, I would recommend getting it already cut up (fresh or frozen) at the grocery store because the whole squash can be hard to cut into. If you do decide to use a whole butternut squash, have an adult help you.

1. **Turn on the oven and prep your baking pan.** Preheat the oven to 350°F. Spray a 9 × 13-inch baking pan with nonstick cooking spray. Have a rimmed baking sheet handy.

2. **Roast your squash.** Toss the butternut squash with the oil on the baking sheet, then spread it out in a single layer. Roast for 25 minutes. Let the squash cool slightly, then transfer it to a large bowl and mash it with a potato masher or fork.

3. **Make the ricotta mixture.** In a medium bowl, lightly beat the egg. Add the ricotta cheese, Parmesan cheese, and ½ cup of the scallions and mix well.

measuring cups

measuring spoons

cutting board and knife

9 × 13-inch baking pan

rimmed baking sheet

large bowl

potato masher or large fork

medium bowl

whisk

wooden spoon

oven mitts

4. **Assemble your lasagna.** Pour 1 can of diced tomatoes into the prepared baking pan and spread them out to cover the bottom of the pan. On top of the tomatoes, place 3 or 4 lasagna noodles side by side to cover the tomatoes. Sprinkle 1 cup of the mozzarella on the noodles, then spoon on half of the mashed butternut squash, and finally spoon on half of the ricotta mixture. Repeat the layers using 3 or 4 more noodles, another 1 cup of the mozzarella, the remaining butternut squash, and the remaining ricotta mixture. Cover the top with the remaining 3 or 4 noodles. Pour the second can of diced tomatoes over the noodles. Sprinkle the remaining 1 cup mozzarella on top.

5. **Bake and let cool.** Bake for 45 to 50 minutes, until the cheese is golden and bubbly. Remove from the oven and sprinkle the remaining ¼ cup scallions over the top. Let cool for 10 minutes before serving.

GET CREATIVE: Herbs like fresh thyme and sage pair really well with butternut squash; try adding them for additional flavor!

QUINOA VEGGIE BOWL

PREP TIME: 20 minutes **COOK TIME:** 15 minutes **SERVES:** 2

Ingredients

1 cup quinoa

2 cups water

1 tablespoon vegetable oil

½ cup chopped broccoli

1 cup chopped bok choy

½ cup sliced mushrooms

1 teaspoon minced
fresh ginger

2 tablespoons soy sauce

1 tablespoon rice vinegar

1 teaspoon pure maple
syrup or agave nectar

Equipment

measuring cups

measuring spoons

cutting board and knife

fine-mesh strainer

medium saucepan

large skillet

wooden spoon

Quinoa is a healthy grain choice because it is high in fiber and protein, but you can use any grain for this recipe—try using wild rice, brown rice, or barley.

1. **Make the quinoa.** Put the quinoa in a fine-mesh strainer and run cool water over it for 30 seconds. Transfer the rinsed quinoa to a medium saucepan and add the 2 cups fresh water. Bring to a boil over medium-high heat, then reduce the heat to low, cover the pan, and cook for 10 to 15 minutes, until all the water is absorbed and the quinoa is tender.

2. **Combine the flavors.** While the quinoa is cooking, heat the vegetable oil in a large skillet over medium heat. Add the broccoli, bok choy, and mushrooms and cook, stirring often, until the vegetables begin to soften, about 5 minutes. Add the ginger, soy sauce, vinegar, and maple syrup or agave and continue to cook, stirring, until the vegetables are cooked, about 5 minutes more.

3. **Assemble the bowls.** Serve the warm vegetables over the quinoa.

GET CREATIVE: Rub a small spoon against the skin of fresh ginger to peel it, then use a zester or grater to mince it. To make the recipe gluten-free, use certified gluten-free quinoa and soy sauce.

NUT-FREE

PESTO PASTA

PREP TIME: 10 minutes **COOK TIME:** 15 minutes **SERVES:** 6

Ingredients

3 cups small pasta (such as penne or elbow macaroni)

½ teaspoon salt, plus a pinch

2½ cups fresh basil leaves

½ cup pine nuts, pistachios, or chopped walnuts

½ cup grated Parmesan cheese

3 garlic cloves, peeled

½ lemon

½ cup extra-virgin olive oil

Equipment

measuring cups

measuring spoons

large pot

colander or strainer

food processor or blender

large spoon

The cool thing about pesto is that you can switch out the pine nuts with pretty much any nut or seed. I love making pesto with walnuts or pistachios. This pesto is a great topping for Easy Flatbread Pizza (page 70) or Leftovers Pasta Salad (page 49).

1. **Boil the pasta.** Fill a large pot halfway with water and bring to a boil over high heat. Add the pasta and a pinch of salt and cook until tender, 8 to 12 minutes. Carefully drain the pasta in a colander, then return the drained pasta to the empty pot.

2. **Make the pesto.** While the pasta is cooking, combine the basil, nuts, Parmesan cheese, garlic, and the ½ teaspoon salt in a food processor or blender. Squeeze in the juice from the lemon half. Blend until smooth. While the machine is running, slowly pour in the olive oil through the opening at the top and blend until smooth.

3. **Combine the pasta and pesto.** Pour the pesto into the pasta and stir to coat. Serve warm.

GET CREATIVE: Try adding different herbs in place of the basil, like parsley, cilantro, or mint.

SIMPLE VEGGIE SOUP

PREP TIME: 30 minutes **COOK TIME:** 1 hour **SERVES:** 6 to 8

Ingredients

1 large onion

2 celery stalks

3 carrots, peeled

3 large or 4 medium red potatoes, well scrubbed

3 garlic cloves

4 cups vegetable broth

2 cups water

2 vegetable bouillon cubes

1 lemon

Salt (optional)

Ground black pepper (optional)

Equipment

measuring cups

peeler

cutting board and knife

large pot

wooden spoon

There is nothing better than a bowl of hot soup on a cold night! You can add any vegetable you like to this soup. You can also add any cooked rice, pasta, or grain. Try experimenting with different ingredients and come up with your own favorite version. This soup goes great with the grilled cheese sandwich on page 48.

1. **Prep your veggies.** Cut the onion, celery, carrots, and potatoes into bite-size pieces. Peel and mince the garlic. Combine all the veggies in a large pot. Add the vegetable broth, water, and bouillon cubes.

2. **Cook your soup.** Cover the pot and cook over low heat for at least 1 hour. (The longer it cooks, the better it will taste!)

3. **Serve and enjoy.** Before serving, cut the lemon in half and squeeze both halves into the pot. Stir, then taste and add salt or pepper, if desired.

GET CREATIVE: If you'd like, you can make this in a slow cooker. Combine all the ingredients in the slow cooker, cover, and cook on low for 3 to 4 hours.

ONE-POT

NUT-FREE

GLUTEN-FREE

EASY FLATBREAD PIZZA

PREP TIME: 1 hour (includes rising time) **COOK TIME:** 20 minutes
SERVES: 8 to 10

Ingredients

2¾ cups all-purpose flour, divided, plus more as needed

1 (¼-ounce) packet instant yeast

1 teaspoon salt

1 teaspoon sugar

½ teaspoon garlic powder

4 tablespoons extra-virgin olive oil, divided

¾ cup warm (not hot!) water

½ cup tomato sauce

1¼ cups shredded mozzarella cheese

You won't believe how easy it is to make homemade pizza dough! The trick to cooking pizza or flatbread is to cook it at a high heat so that the crust cooks quickly. Unlike regular round pizza, this flatbread will be a rectangle.

1. **Make the dough.** In a large bowl, whisk together 1½ cups of the flour, the yeast, salt, sugar, and garlic powder. Add 2 tablespoons of the olive oil and the warm water, and mix with a wooden spoon until combined. Gradually add the remaining 1¼ cups flour and mix well. If the dough seems sticky, add 1 to 2 more tablespoons flour until the dough is smooth and pulls away from the sides of the bowl as you mix it.

2. **Knead the dough.** Scatter flour all over a clean work surface to prevent sticking. Put the dough on the flour and knead with your hands for 8 to 10 minutes, as if you are playing with Play-Doh, then form a big ball.

3. **Let the dough rise.** Pour the remaining 2 tablespoons olive oil into a clean bowl and spread it around with a spatula. Put the dough ball in the bowl and turn the ball in the bowl so it is covered in olive oil. Cover the bowl with plastic wrap and set it in a warm place for 30 to 45 minutes to rise.

NUT-FREE

Equipment

measuring cups

measuring spoons

2 large bowls

whisk

wooden spoon

spatula

plastic wrap

rimmed baking sheet

parchment paper

rolling pin

fork

oven mitts

4. **Turn on the oven and prep your baking sheet.** While the dough is rising, preheat the oven to 425°F. Line a rimmed baking sheet with parchment paper.

5. **Make the flatbread.** Sprinkle more flour on your work surface and dump the dough on top. Roll the dough into a large rectangle with a rolling pin. Transfer the dough rectangle to the prepared baking sheet. Use a fork to poke 10 or 12 holes all over the dough. Spread the tomato sauce on the dough, going almost all the way to the edges, then scatter the cheese on top.

6. **Bake the pizza and enjoy.** Bake for 12 to 16 minutes, until the crust is golden and the cheese is bubbling. Let cool slightly before slicing and serving.

GET CREATIVE: You can top this pizza dough with whatever you want! Try adding different sauces (like the pesto on page 68) and your favorite sliced vegetables, such as mushrooms and bell peppers.

SUPER GREENS STEW WITH GARLIC BREAD

PREP TIME: 15 minutes **COOK TIME:** 15 minutes **SERVES:** 4 to 6

Ingredients

½ loaf rustic bread

4 tablespoons extra-virgin olive oil, divided

3 garlic cloves, minced, divided

1 (15-ounce) can white beans

½ cup chopped onion

1 (15-ounce) can diced tomatoes

8 cups stemmed and chopped kale, collard greens, and/or spinach

½ teaspoon salt

1 lemon

Equipment

measuring spoons

cutting board and knife

measuring cups

rimmed baking sheet

small bowl

small spoon

colander or strainer

large skillet

wooden spoon

oven mitts

There are so many leafy greens that are great to cook with—and good for you, too! Choose your favorite to whip up into a stew to enjoy with a warm piece of garlic bread.

1. **Turn on the oven.** Preheat the oven to 350°F.

2. **Make the garlic bread.** Slice the bread and lay out the slices on a rimmed baking sheet. In a small bowl, mix 2 tablespoons of the olive oil and half of the minced garlic. Use a small spoon to drizzle the garlic oil over the bread. Bake for 10 minutes.

3. **Drain the beans.** Drain the beans in a colander and rinse under cool running water.

4. **Make the stew.** Heat the remaining 2 tablespoons olive oil in a large skillet over medium heat. Add the onion and cook, stirring, for 3 minutes. Pour in the can of tomatoes, chopped greens, remaining garlic, and salt. Cut the lemon in half and squeeze in the juice. Cook, stirring, until the greens turn bright green, then add the beans and cook for another 2 minutes. Remove the stew from the heat and serve with the garlic bread.

CRUSTLESS PORTOBELLO MUSHROOM PIZZA

PREP TIME: 20 minutes **COOK TIME:** 45 minutes **SERVES:** 4

Ingredients

4 portobello mushrooms

3 tablespoons extra-virgin olive oil, divided

½ medium onion, diced

1 cup diced tomato (fresh or canned)

1 garlic clove, minced

1 teaspoon salt

1 cup shredded mozzarella cheese

½ bell pepper (any color), thinly sliced

1 (4-ounce) can sliced black olives, drained

Equipment

measuring spoons

cutting board and knife

measuring cups

rimmed baking sheet

parchment paper

large skillet

wooden spoon

oven mitts

> In this recipe, we'll make personal-size mini pizzas. Instead of pizza dough, though, we'll use portobello mushrooms!

1. **Turn on the oven and prep your baking sheet.** Preheat the oven to 350°F. Line a rimmed baking sheet with parchment paper.

2. **Prep the mushrooms.** Wash the portobello mushrooms and pat dry. Remove the mushroom stems and finely chop the stems.

3. **Cook the topping.** Heat 2 tablespoons of the olive oil in a large skillet over medium heat. Add the onion and mushroom stems and cook, stirring, for 5 minutes. Add the tomato and garlic, turn the heat down to low, and cook, stirring occasionally, for 20 minutes.

4. **Assemble the mushroom pizzas.** Rub the mushroom caps with the remaining 1 tablespoon olive oil and season with the salt. Place on the prepared baking sheet, rounded side down. Spoon 2 to 3 tablespoons of the tomato mixture onto the center of each mushroom, then top each with ¼ cup of the cheese. Add the bell pepper and olives on top.

5. **Bake and enjoy.** Bake for 20 minutes. Let cool slightly and serve warm.

GET CREATIVE: You can use thickly sliced eggplant instead of portobello mushrooms, if you prefer.

NUT-FREE

GLUTEN-FREE

VEGGIE FRIED RICE

PREP TIME: 10 minutes **COOK TIME:** 10 minutes **SERVES:** 4 to 6

30-MINUTE

ONE-POT

NUT-FREE

Ingredients

2 large eggs

1 tablespoon toasted sesame oil

3 cups cooked rice, chilled

1 cup frozen peas and carrots

2 garlic cloves, minced

3 tablespoons soy sauce

¼ cup sliced scallions (white and light green parts)

Equipment

measuring spoons

measuring cups

cutting board and knife

small bowl

whisk

wok or large skillet

spatula

This is the perfect recipe to make with left-over rice, since fried rice is easier to cook when the rice is cold.

1. **Prep the eggs.** Crack the eggs into a small bowl and lightly whisk them.

2. **Stir-fry the ingredients.** Heat the sesame oil in a wok or large skillet over medium heat. Add the rice, peas and carrots, garlic, and soy sauce and cook, stirring, until everything is heated through, 5 to 7 minutes. Add the eggs and stir, breaking up the eggs into small pieces. Once the eggs are cooked through (they'll look like scrambled eggs), remove the pan from the heat. Stir in the scallions and serve warm.

GET CREATIVE: If you like spicy foods, you can add sweet chili sauce or red pepper flakes to this recipe. To make the recipe gluten-free, use certified gluten-free soy sauce.

BUILD YOUR SKILLS
HOW TO MAKE A ROUX

In this chapter, we'll need to make a roux for the Baked Broccoli Mac and Cheese (page 76). A roux is a mixture of flour and butter that is often used to thicken sauces and soups and to add flavor. When making a roux, you first melt butter in a pan and then add flour. Make sure to stir continually in the shape of the number 8 with a wooden spoon or spatula for 3 to 5 minutes. It's important to keep stirring for even cooking and to prevent sticking or burning. For the mac and cheese, we'll be making a light roux, also called a white roux, which simply means it is light in color. You will know it's done when it starts to puff slightly.

BAKED BROCCOLI MAC AND CHEESE

PREP TIME: 15 minutes **COOK TIME:** 1 hour **SERVES:** 8 to 12

Ingredients

Nonstick cooking spray

2 heads broccoli

3 cups elbow macaroni

1 tablespoon salt

4 tablespoons (½ stick) unsalted butter

3 tablespoons all-purpose flour

2 cups milk

3½ cups grated cheddar cheese, divided

¾ cup bread crumbs

NUT-FREE

This recipe makes a deliciously creamy, gooey baked mac and cheese topped with crunchy bread crumbs. If you do not like broccoli, you can use cauliflower or peas instead.

1. **Turn on the oven and prep your baking pan.** Preheat the oven to 350°F. Spray a 9 × 13-inch baking pan with nonstick cooking spray.

2. **Prep the broccoli.** Cut off the broccoli stems and leaves and discard. Cut the broccoli florets into bite-size pieces.

3. **Make the macaroni.** Fill a large pot halfway with water and bring to a boil over high heat. Add the macaroni and salt and cook for 5 minutes. Carefully drain the pasta in a colander.

4. **Make a cheesy sauce.** Melt the butter in a large saucepan over medium heat. Whisk in the flour to create a roux (see page 75). While whisking continually, slowly pour in the milk. Gradually add 3 cups of the cheese, stirring with a wooden spoon to melt the cheese.

Equipment

measuring cups

measuring spoons

9 × 13-inch baking pan

cutting board and knife

large pot

colander or strainer

large saucepan

whisk

wooden spoon

oven mitts

5. **Combine the flavors.** Add the chopped broccoli and cook, stirring, for 4 minutes. Remove the pan from the heat and gently stir in the drained macaroni.

6. **Bake and enjoy.** Transfer the mac and cheese mixture to the prepared baking pan. Scatter the remaining ½ cup grated cheese and the bread crumbs all over the top. Bake for 40 to 45 minutes, until golden brown. Serve warm.

GET CREATIVE: Try adding any of the following spices to this dish: 1 teaspoon garlic powder, ½ teaspoon freshly ground black pepper, ½ teaspoon paprika. To make your dish look fancy, top it with finely sliced scallion greens or chopped fresh parsley to add a bit of color and freshness!

THREE-BEAN CHILI

PREP TIME: 10 minutes **COOK TIME:** 50 minutes **SERVES:** 8 to 10

Ingredients

1 (15-ounce) can black beans

1 (15-ounce) can pinto beans

1 (15-ounce) can kidney beans

1 large onion

3 tablespoons extra-virgin olive oil

2 (15-ounce) cans diced tomatoes

1 tablespoon chili powder

2 teaspoons ground cumin

2 teaspoons salt

Equipment

measuring spoons

colander or strainer

cutting board and knife

large pot

wooden spoon

Like many soups and stews, chili gets better the longer it cooks and also often tastes even better the next day, after the flavors have had time to mix. This chili is excellent with Classic Cornbread (page 37).

1. **Prep the ingredients.** Dump all the beans into a colander and rinse under cool running water. Chop the onion.

2. **Cook the chili.** In a large pot, heat the olive oil over medium-low heat. Add the onion and cook, stirring, for 5 minutes. Pour in the cans of tomatoes and add all the beans. Add the chili powder, cumin, and salt and stir well. Cover the pot, turn the heat down to low, and cook for 45 minutes. Serve warm.

GET CREATIVE: Try topping your chili with sour cream or plain Greek-style yogurt, shredded cheese, diced avocado, fresh herbs like cilantro or parsley, chopped onion or scallion, or crushed-up tortilla chips. You can also make this recipe in a slow cooker. Combine all the ingredients in the slow cooker, cover, and cook on Low for 3 to 4 hours.

STUFFED POTATO TACOS

PREP TIME: 15 minutes **COOK TIME:** 40 minutes **SERVES:** 4

Ingredients

2 large potatoes (any kind), well scrubbed

2 tablespoons salted butter, at room temperature

1 (15-ounce) can black beans

2 tomatoes

1 avocado

2 scallions

¼ cup fresh cilantro leaves

Pinch salt

Pinch ground black pepper

1 cup shredded cheddar cheese

¼ cup sliced black olives

½ cup sour cream (optional)

1 lime

Did you know that there are more than 4,000 different types of potatoes found around the world? For this recipe, you can use any kind of potato you like—such as sweet potatoes or russet potatoes—as long as they're large enough.

1. **Turn on the oven and prep your potatoes.** Preheat the oven to 400°F. Use a fork to poke holes 6 to 8 times all over the potatoes. Cut each potato in half lengthwise. Rub the potato halves all over with the butter and put on a rimmed baking sheet.

2. **Bake the potatoes.** Bake for 20 minutes, then remove the baking sheet from the oven and carefully flip the potatoes over. Bake for another 20 minutes.

3. **Prep the filling.** While the potatoes are baking, drain the beans in a colander and rinse under cool running water. Chop the tomatoes. Cut the avocado into cubes according to the instructions on page 16. Thinly slice the scallions, using just the white and light green parts. Roughly chop the cilantro.

NUT-FREE

GLUTEN-FREE

(Continued)

Equipment

measuring spoons

measuring cups

fork

cutting board and knife

rimmed baking sheet

colander or strainer

oven mitts

spoon

4. **Stuff the potatoes.** Remove the potatoes from the oven and season with the salt and pepper. Press down with a spoon to make an indentation in the middle of each potato half. Fill the indentations with beans, then top with cheese, tomatoes, avocado, scallions, olives, cilantro, and sour cream (if using). Cut the lime into 4 wedges and let each person squeeze the juice over the top before enjoying.

GET CREATIVE: You can easily make this a vegan dish by replacing the butter with vegetable oil and leaving out the cheese and sour cream.

TOFU BANH MI SANDWICH

PREP TIME: 30 minutes **COOK TIME:** 40 minutes **MAKES:** 4 sandwiches

Ingredients

2 limes

4 tablespoons agave nectar, divided

2 teaspoons salt, divided

1 (10- to 12-ounce) package extra-firm tofu

1 carrot

½ small red onion

1 cucumber

1 cup vinegar (any kind)

½ cup hot water

1 long baguette

Small bunch fresh cilantro

Equipment

measuring spoons

measuring cups

rimmed baking sheet

parchment paper

cutting board and knife

medium bowl

small jar

oven mitts

The banh mi sandwich was created in Vietnam in the 1950s. It became popular in the United States in the 1970s. Served on a baguette, it's a hearty sandwich that includes salty, sweet, sour, and spicy flavors. In this recipe, we'll learn how to quickly pickle vegetables, and we'll replace the meat usually found in a banh mi with tofu.

1. **Turn on the oven and prep your baking sheet.** Preheat the oven to 350°F. Line a rimmed baking sheet with parchment paper.

2. **Make the marinade for the tofu.** Cut the limes in half and squeeze the juice into a medium bowl. Add 1 tablespoon of the agave and 1 teaspoon of the salt.

3. **Marinate and bake the tofu.** Open the tofu package and drain off the liquid. Cut the tofu into ½-inch-thick slices and gently press down on each slice to release any extra liquid. Dip each slice into the marinade, covering both sides, and place on the prepared baking sheet in a single layer. Bake for 20 minutes, flip the slices, and bake for another 20 minutes.

4. **Prep the veggies.** While the tofu is baking, cut the carrot, onion, and cucumber into thin matchsticks (julienne).

(Continued)

5. **Pickle the veggies.** In a small jar, combine the vinegar, hot water, remaining 3 tablespoons agave, and remaining 1 teaspoon salt. Add the carrot and onion, cover the jar, and let sit until the tofu is done (the veggies should sit for at least 30 minutes).

6. **Assemble the sandwich.** Cut the baguette into 4 pieces, then slice each piece in half. Fill the sandwiches with tofu, pickled carrot and onion, cucumber, and cilantro leaves.

GET CREATIVE: If you like spicy food, you can add thinly sliced jalapeños to your sandwich. You can also use this pickling technique to make a cucumber and onion salad.

ENCHILADA CASSEROLE

PREP TIME: 15 minutes **COOK TIME:** 40 minutes **SERVES:** 9

Ingredients

Nonstick cooking spray

2 (16-ounce) jars
salsa verde

2 garlic cloves, minced

½ cup plain
Greek-style yogurt

½ teaspoon ground cumin

2 (15-ounce) cans black or
pinto beans

12 corn tortillas

1 cup frozen corn, thawed

3 cups shredded cheddar,
Monterey Jack or Mexican
blend cheese, divided

Equipment

cutting board and knife

measuring cups

measuring spoons

8-inch square baking pan

large bowl

whisk

colander

aluminum foil

oven mitts

Enchiladas come from Mexico, where the tradition of rolling tortillas around other food started all the way back in the 15th century! Today enchiladas are made many different ways. This dish has all the flavors of enchiladas in green sauce, but instead of rolling tortillas, we'll layer them to make a casserole.

1. **Turn on the oven and prep your baking pan.** Preheat the oven to 375°F. Spray an 8-inch square baking pan with nonstick cooking spray.

2. **Make the sauce.** In a large bowl, whisk the salsa verde, garlic, yogurt, and cumin until blended.

3. **Prep the beans.** Drain the beans in a colander and rinse under cool running water.

4. **Assemble the casserole.** Pour ½ cup of sauce into the prepared baking pan. Place 4 corn tortillas in the prepared pan. Cover the tortillas with half of the beans, half of the corn, and 1 cup of the cheese. Repeat the layers with another 4 tortillas and the remaining beans, remaining corn, and another 1 cup of the cheese. Cover the top layer with the remaining 4 tortillas. Pour the remaining sauce on top, then sprinkle with the remaining 1 cup cheese.

5. **Bake the casserole.** Cover the pan with foil. Bake for 30 minutes, then remove the pan from the oven and remove the foil. Continue baking for 7 to 10 minutes, until the cheese is melted and golden.

SAVORY GALETTE

PREP TIME: 1½ hours (includes chilling time)
COOK TIME: 55 minutes **SERVES:** 8

Ingredients

FOR THE CRUST

1¼ cups all-purpose flour, plus more for dusting

8 tablespoons (1 stick) cold salted butter, cut into small cubes

¼ cup ice water

1 large egg yolk (see page 92)

FOR THE FILLING

3 small zucchini

½ red onion

1 tablespoon extra-virgin olive oil

1 teaspoon fresh thyme leaves

1 teaspoon fresh oregano leaves (optional)

1 large garlic clove, minced

3 cups chopped fresh tomatoes

Pinch salt

Pinch ground black pepper

⅓ cup shredded mozzarella cheese

⅓ cup grated Parmesan cheese

> The word *galette* means flat cake! It's a term used in French cooking to describe a pie-like pastry that is made without a pie pan. Galettes can be sweet or savory. To save time, use store-bought pie dough that you roll out.

TO MAKE THE CRUST

1. **Make the dough.** Combine the flour and butter in a large bowl. Use a fork to mix the butter into the flour until you have what looks like crumbs about the size of raisins. Pour the ice water into the bowl, then mix with your fingers until the dough starts to stick together.

2. **Let the dough rest.** On a lightly floured surface, roll the dough into a ball using your hands and then flatten the ball into a disc. Return the dough to the bowl and cover with plastic wrap. Chill it in the fridge for at least 1 hour.

TO MAKE THE FILLING

3. **Prep the veggies.** Chop the zucchini and onion.

4. **Cook the filling.** Heat the oil in a large skillet over medium heat. Add the onion, thyme, and oregano (if using) and cook, stirring, for 2 to 3 minutes. Add the garlic and tomatoes and cook, stirring occasionally, for 10 minutes. Add the zucchini and cook until slightly softened, about 5 minutes. Add the salt and pepper.

(Continued)

NUT-FREE

Equipment

measuring cups

cutting board and knife

measuring spoons

large bowl

fork

plastic wrap

large skillet

wooden spoon

rimmed baking sheet

parchment paper

rolling pin

pastry brush

oven mitts

5. **Let cool.** Remove the skillet from the heat and let cool slightly.

TO ASSEMBLE AND BAKE

6. **Turn on the oven and prep your baking sheet.** Preheat the oven to 375°F. Line a rimmed baking sheet with parchment paper.

7. **Roll out the dough.** Scatter flour all over a clean work surface to prevent sticking. Take the dough out of the fridge and put it on the flour. Use a rolling pin to roll out the dough into a round about 12 inches across. Place on the prepared baking sheet.

8. **Add the cheese.** Take the filling and add half of the mozzarella and half of the Parmesan. Mix well.

9. **Assemble the galette.** Spoon the filling onto the center of the dough round, leaving a border of 2½ to 3 inches of dough empty around the edges. Sprinkle the remaining mozzarella and Parmesan on top of the filling. Fold over the edges of the dough toward the center, as if you're wrapping a package, leaving some of the filling showing in the center.

10. **Bake the galette.** Brush the egg yolk all over the exposed dough. Bake for about 35 minutes, or until golden. Transfer to a wire rack and let cool for at least 20 minutes before serving.

GET CREATIVE: To get a flaky dough, make sure you do not overdo it when you roll it out because that would make the dough become tough.

ULTIMATE VEGGIE BURGER

PREP TIME: 40 minutes **COOK TIME:** 1 hour **MAKES:** 6 to 8 burgers

NUT-FREE

Ingredients

¼ cup red split lentils

1 small onion

8 mushrooms

1 beet

2 tablespoons vegetable oil

4 tablespoons rolled oats

1 (15-ounce) can chickpeas

1 large egg

¼ cup coconut aminos

½ teaspoon salt

Who doesn't love a good burger? These veggie burgers are full of texture and flavor, just like ones with meat. You can use this recipe to make mini sliders or full-size burgers, and you can eat them on a bun or on their own.

1. **Turn on the oven and prep your baking sheet.** Preheat the oven to 400°F. Line a rimmed baking sheet with parchment paper.

2. **Soak the lentils.** Put the lentils in a small bowl, pour in enough water to cover them, and let soak for 20 to 30 minutes.

3. **Prep the veggies.** While the lentils are soaking, quarter the onion and halve the mushrooms. Peel and finely chop the beet. (Be sure to wash your hands well after handling the beet as it will stain! You might want to wear an apron if you have one.) Put the onion, mushrooms, and beet in separate areas on the prepared baking sheet. Drizzle them with the vegetable oil.

4. **Roast the veggies.** Roast for 12 minutes. Remove the onion and mushrooms with tongs or a spatula and transfer them to the cutting board to cool slightly. Return the beets to the oven and roast for another 12 minutes. Remove the beets from the oven. Reduce the oven temperature to 350°F.

measuring cups

measuring spoons

rimmed baking sheet

parchment paper

small bowl

cutting board and knife

peeler

tongs or spatula

food processor

colander or strainer

whisk

large bowl

large spoon

oven mitts

5. **Blend the ingredients.** Put the oats and roasted beets in a food processor and blend until smooth. Drain the soaked lentils in a colander and add to the food processor. Drain the chickpeas in the colander, rinse under cool running water, and add to the food processor. Pulse the mixture 8 to 10 times—you do not want to fully blend the chickpeas and lentils.

6. **Combine all the flavors.** Whisk the egg in a large bowl. Finely chop the roasted onion and mushrooms and add them to the bowl. Add the beet mixture to the bowl. Add the coconut aminos and salt and mix everything together well.

7. **Make the patties.** Place a clean sheet of parchment on the same baking sheet. Use your hands to scoop out the burger mixture. Form a ball, then press into a patty shape and put on the prepared baking sheet. You should be able to make 6 to 8 burgers.

8. **Bake and enjoy.** Bake the burgers for 35 minutes. Enjoy warm.

GET CREATIVE: Make this into a cheeseburger by taking the burgers out of the oven after 30 minutes and adding a slice of cheese (any kind) on top. Return to the oven for an additional 5 minutes. Serve the burgers on buns with all your favorite toppings or on a bed of lettuce. To make the recipe gluten-free, use certified gluten-free oats.

CHAPTER 6

Desserts and Treats

BUILD YOUR SKILLS
HOW TO SEPARATE EGGS

Learning how to separate an egg is an important skill because some recipes call for just an egg yolk (as in the Savory Galette, page 85) and other recipes call for just an egg white (as in the Coconut Macaroons, opposite page). It might seem tricky at first, but you will get better at it with practice. First, crack the side of the egg gently on your countertop. Hold the egg over a bowl and carefully separate the two halves, so you are holding one in each hand. Gently pour the yolk from one half of the eggshell to the other, letting the white drip down into the bowl. Be careful not to break the yolk! Keep doing this until you're left with just the yolk in one half of the eggshell and all the white is in the bowl. You can store whichever part you don't need in an airtight container in the fridge for up to 4 days, until you need it—just add it to the bowl the next time you make scrambled eggs.

COCONUT MACAROONS

PREP TIME: 15 minutes **COOK TIME:** 18 minutes **MAKES:** 18 to 24 cookies

Ingredients

2 large egg whites (see page 92)

⅔ cup sugar

½ teaspoon salt

1 teaspoon vanilla extract

2⅔ cups dried shredded coconut

Equipment

measuring cups

measuring spoons

rimmed baking sheet

parchment paper

electric mixer

small spoon

spatula

large spoon

oven mitts

> These coconut macaroons are a flourless cookie, so they are naturally gluten-free!

1. **Turn on the oven and prep your baking sheet.** Preheat the oven to 350°F. Line a rimmed baking sheet with parchment paper.

2. **Whip the egg whites.** Using an electric mixer, beat the egg whites, sugar, and salt together at high speed for about 1 minute. You'll know they're ready when you dip a spoon in and the egg whites make a sturdy peak (like a mountain peak) on the back.

3. **Combine the flavors.** Add the vanilla and coconut and stir gently and slowly, flipping over the mixture with a spatula as if you are folding it. (That's why this is called "folding in" an ingredient.)

4. **Create the cookies.** Use a large spoon to scoop 2 tablespoons of dough per cookie and place on the prepared baking sheet. Use your fingers to form each mound of dough into a little mountain peak.

5. **Bake and enjoy.** Bake for 18 minutes, or until the cookies turn light golden. Enjoy hot out of the oven or at room temperature.

GET CREATIVE: If you want to be fancy, try dipping the finished and completely cooled cookies into melted chocolate.

5-INGREDIENT

GLUTEN-FREE

DOUBLE CHOCOLATE CHEWY BROWNIES

PREP TIME: 15 minutes **COOK TIME:** 30 to 35 minutes **MAKES:** 24 brownies

Ingredients

Nonstick cooking spray

1 cup (2 sticks) salted butter

1¼ cups all-purpose flour

½ teaspoon baking powder

1½ cups granulated sugar

½ cup packed dark brown sugar

¾ cup cocoa powder

4 large eggs

½ cup chocolate chips

Equipment

measuring cups

measuring spoons

9 × 13-inch baking pan

small saucepan

medium bowl

whisk

large bowl

spatula

toothpick

oven mitts

> Some people prefer their brownies more like cake and other people prefer them more like fudge. If you like them cakey and crumbly, cook them for the full 35 minutes. If you like them chewy and gooey, take them out after 30 minutes. It's up to you!

1. **Turn on the oven and prep your baking pan.** Preheat the oven to 350°F. Spray a 9 × 13-inch baking pan with nonstick cooking spray.

2. **Melt the butter.** Put the butter in a small saucepan and let it melt over low heat. Set aside to cool slightly.

3. **Whisk the dry ingredients.** In a medium bowl, whisk together the flour and baking powder.

4. **Whisk the wet ingredients.** When the butter has cooled slightly, pour it into a large bowl and add the granulated sugar, brown sugar, cocoa powder, and eggs. Whisk everything together until smooth.

5. **Combine the ingredients.** Gradually mix the dry ingredients into the wet ingredients until well combined. Stir in the chocolate chips.

6. **Bake and enjoy.** Pour the batter into the prepared baking pan and bake for 30 to 35 minutes, until a toothpick poked in the center comes out clean or with just a few crumbs on it. Let cool before slicing and serving.

NUT-FREE

PEACH CRUMBLE

PREP TIME: 45 minutes (includes resting time)
COOK TIME: 45 minutes **SERVES:** 8

Ingredients

5½ cups frozen peach slices, thawed (or use fresh peaches, peeled, pitted, and sliced)

1 cup packed light brown sugar

¼ cup tapioca powder

2 teaspoons ground cinnamon, divided

Nonstick cooking spray

5 tablespoons cold salted butter, cubed

¼ cup granulated sugar

3 tablespoons all-purpose flour

3 tablespoons rolled oats

3 tablespoons sliced almonds

3 tablespoons chopped walnuts

Equipment

measuring cups

measuring spoons

cutting board and knife

large bowl

9-inch square baking pan

medium bowl

fork

oven mitts

> This is called a crumble because instead of a pie crust for the topping, it has a delicious and sweet crumbly topping.

1. **Combine the flavors.** In a large bowl, toss together the peaches, brown sugar, tapioca, and 1 teaspoon of the cinnamon. Let the mixture sit at room temperature for 30 minutes.

2. **Turn on the oven and prep your baking pan.** Preheat the oven to 350°F. Spray a 9-inch square baking pan with nonstick cooking spray.

3. **Make the topping.** In a medium bowl, combine the butter, granulated sugar, flour, oats, almonds, walnuts, and the remaining 1 teaspoon cinnamon. Mix with a fork or your fingers until everything starts to stick together to create a crumbly mixture.

4. **Assemble and bake.** Pour the peaches into the prepared baking pan and scatter the crumble mixture all over the top. Bake for 45 minutes, or until the juices from the peaches are bubbling and the topping is golden. Let cool slightly and serve.

GET CREATIVE: To make this gluten-free, use almond flour or gluten-free flour and certified gluten-free oats. To make this nut-free, skip the nuts and double the flour for the topping. Try adding mixed berries to the peaches, or substituting apples or pears.

ALMOND SHORTBREAD COOKIES

PREP TIME: 15 minutes **COOK TIME:** 1 hour **MAKES:** 12 cookies

Ingredients

Nonstick cooking spray

1 cup (2 sticks) salted butter, at room temperature

½ cup confectioners' sugar

¼ cup granulated sugar

2 cups all-purpose flour

¼ cup sliced almonds

Equipment

measuring cups

8-inch square baking pan

electric mixer

spoon

oven mitts

Classic shortbread is a great cookie to make when you don't have milk, eggs, baking soda, or baking powder in the house. Its sweet buttery flavor makes it the perfect cookie for the holidays or an afternoon tea party.

1. **Turn on the oven and prep your baking pan.** Preheat the oven to 300°F. Spray an 8-inch square baking pan with nonstick cooking spray.

2. **Mix all the ingredients.** Using an electric mixer, mix the butter, confectioners' sugar, and granulated sugar on medium speed until fluffy. Gradually add the flour until incorporated. Add the sliced almonds and use a spoon to mix them in.

3. **Bake and enjoy.** Transfer the dough to the prepared baking pan. Press it into the corners and smooth the top. Bake for 1 hour. Cool completely, then cut into 12 rectangles to serve.

GET CREATIVE: To make these cookies nut-free, replace the almonds with 1 teaspoon grated lemon zest or 1 tablespoon vanilla extract.

5-INGREDIENT

COOKIES AND CREAM FROZEN YOGURT

PREP TIME: 4½ hours (includes freezing time) **SERVES:** 6 to 8

Ingredients

2 cups vanilla Greek-style yogurt

1 (8-ounce) package cream cheese, at room temperature

3 tablespoons pure maple syrup

18 (nut-free) cookies (any kind you like)

¼ cup chocolate chips

Equipment

measuring cups

measuring spoons

food processor or blender

freezer-safe container

large spoon or spatula

Everyone loves this frozen treat! It comes together easily, and you don't even need an ice cream maker.

1. **Blend.** In a food processor or blender, blend the yogurt and cream cheese until smooth and creamy. Add the maple syrup and blend until well mixed. Transfer the mixture to a freezer-safe container with a lid.

2. **Add some crunch.** Break up the cookies with your hands so that you have a mix of large and small pieces. Mix the cookie pieces and chocolate chips into the yogurt using a large spoon or spatula.

3. **Freeze.** Cover the container and freeze for at least 4 hours.

GET CREATIVE: Try using different flavor combinations, such as lemon yogurt with gingersnaps. If you like, add frozen fruit, too—for example, you could use a combination of strawberry yogurt, frozen sliced strawberries, and chocolate cookies.

CREAMY CHEESECAKE

PREP TIME: 2½ hours (including chilling time)
COOK TIME: 45 to 50 minutes **SERVES:** 8

Ingredients

FOR THE CRUST

Nonstick cooking spray

6 tablespoons (¾ stick) unsalted butter

9 full sheets (18 squares) cinnamon graham crackers

2 tablespoons light brown sugar

FOR THE FILLING

2 (8-ounce) packages cream cheese, at room temperature

¾ cup granulated sugar

½ cup plain Greek-style yogurt

1 teaspoon vanilla extract

2 large eggs

Equipment

measuring spoons

measuring cups

pie pan

small saucepan

large zip-top bag

rolling pin

electric mixer

oven mitts

This creamy cheesecake needs to be chilled before serving, so plan ahead. You can top it with fresh fruit, whipped cream, or chocolate sauce. The strawberry topping from the shortcake on page 104 also works great here!

TO MAKE THE CRUST

1. **Turn on the oven and prep your pie pan.** Preheat the oven to 350°F. Spray a pie pan with nonstick cooking spray.

2. **Prepare the crust.** Put the butter in a small saucepan and let it melt over low heat. Set aside to cool slightly. Put the graham crackers in a large zip-top bag, press out the air, and seal the bag. Use a rolling pin to crush the graham crackers until they are like sand. Add the brown sugar and melted butter and seal the bag again. Squish the bag with your hands to mix everything together. Pour the crust mixture into the prepared pie pan. Spread it out so it covers the whole bottom and press it into an even layer.

TO MAKE THE FILLING

3. **Blend the filling and fill the crust.** Using an
   electric mixer, blend the cream cheese, granulated
   sugar, yogurt, and vanilla on medium speed until
   smooth and creamy. Add the eggs, one at a time, and
   blend until incorporated. Pour the filling over the
   graham cracker crust.

TO FINISH THE CHEESECAKE

4. **Bake and chill the cake.** Bake for 45 to 50 minutes,
   until the center looks like it has set. Let the cake cool
   slightly at room temperature, then put it in the fridge
   for at least 2 hours to chill before serving.

GET CREATIVE: To make cheesecake squares, use
a 9-inch square baking pan instead of a pie pan.

VERY VANILLA CUPCAKES WITH FROSTING

PREP TIME: 1 hour (includes cooling time)
COOK TIME: 20 minutes **MAKES:** 12 cupcakes

Ingredients

FOR THE CUPCAKES

8 tablespoons (1 stick) salted butter, at room temperature

1 cup granulated sugar

3 large eggs

1 tablespoon vanilla extract

1½ cups all-purpose flour

2 teaspoons baking powder

½ cup milk

FOR THE FROSTING

8 tablespoons (1 stick) unsalted butter, at room temperature

3½ cups confectioners' sugar

⅓ cup milk

2 teaspoons vanilla extract

¼ cup rainbow sprinkles

These cupcakes are moist and sweet and make a delicious treat for any special occasion. You can turn them into confetti cupcakes by adding colorful sprinkles to the batter and frosting.

TO MAKE THE CUPCAKES

1. **Turn on the oven and prep your muffin tin.** Preheat the oven to 350°F. Line a muffin tin with cupcake liners.

2. **Mix the butter and sugar.** Combine the butter and granulated sugar in a large bowl and mix well. Add the eggs, one at a time, and the vanilla and mix until smooth.

3. **Mix it up.** In a small bowl, whisk together the flour and baking powder. Add the dry ingredients to the wet ingredients. Add the milk and mix until smooth.

4. **Bake and cool.** Pour the batter into the prepared muffin tin. Bake for 20 minutes, or until a toothpick poked in the center of a cupcake comes out clean. Remove from the oven and set aside to cool completely.

measuring cups

measuring spoons

muffin tin

cupcake liners

2 large bowls

large spoon

small bowl

whisk

toothpick

oven mitts

electric mixer

large zip-top bag

TO FROST THE CUPCAKES

5. **Make the frosting.** While the cupcakes cool, in a large bowl, use an electric mixer to beat the butter until fluffy. Then add the confectioners' sugar, milk, and vanilla and beat until smooth and creamy.

6. **Frost the cupcakes and enjoy.** Transfer the frosting to a large zip-top bag, press out the air, and seal the bag. Cut off one bottom corner of the bag (just a little bit) to create a piping bag. Squeeze the frosting out of the hole you made and onto the cupcakes. Top each cupcake with some sprinkles.

GET CREATIVE: Want to flavor your frosting? Try adding ¼ cup of your favorite jam, peanut butter, or cocoa powder.

STRAWBERRY SHORTCAKE

PREP TIME: 1 hour **COOK TIME:** 20 minutes **SERVES:** 6 to 8

Ingredients

FOR THE BISCUITS

½ cup heavy cream

½ cup plain
Greek-style yogurt

2 teaspoons vanilla extract

2 cups all-purpose flour,
plus more for dusting

3 tablespoons sugar

1¼ teaspoons
baking powder

½ teaspoon baking soda

8 tablespoons (1 stick)
very cold salted butter, cut
into small cubes

FOR THE
STRAWBERRY
TOPPING

4 cups sliced strawberries

½ lemon

¼ cup sugar

¼ teaspoon salt

FOR THE
WHIPPED CREAM

1 cup heavy cream

2 tablespoons sugar

> Strawberry shortcake is made up of a warm biscuit, sliced strawberries, and whipped cream and is often enjoyed in the summer.

TO MAKE THE BISCUITS

1. **Turn on the oven and prep your baking sheet.** Preheat the oven to 400°F. Line a rimmed baking sheet with parchment paper.

2. **Mix the wet ingredients.** In a medium bowl, whisk together the cream, yogurt, and vanilla.

3. **Mix the dry ingredients and wet ingredients.** In a large bowl, whisk together the flour, sugar, baking powder, and baking soda. Add the butter and mix it in with a fork until it looks like coarse sand. Push the dough to the sides of the bowl to create a hole in the center. Pour the wet ingredients into the hole and mix it all together with a spatula. Be careful not to overmix.

4. **Roll and cut out the biscuits.** Scatter flour all over a clean work space to prevent sticking. Transfer the dough to the flour and roll it out with a rolling pin to about an 8 × 12-inch rectangle. Cut the dough into 4 even pieces, stack the pieces to create a tower, then flatten the tower with your hands. This will create a flaky texture when your biscuits bake. Roll the dough out again into an 8 × 12-inch rectangle. Cut out 6 to 8 square biscuits with a knife or use a round biscuit cutter if you have one.

Equipment

measuring cups

measuring spoons

cutting board and knife

rimmed baking sheet

parchment paper

medium bowl

2 large bowls

whisk

fork

spatula

rolling pin

biscuit cutter

electric mixer

oven mitts

large spoon

5. **Bake the biscuits.** Put the biscuits on the prepared baking sheet and bake for 17 to 20 minutes, until golden brown.

TO MAKE THE TOPPING AND ASSEMBLE

6. **Prep the strawberries.** Meanwhile, put the sliced strawberries in another large bowl. Squeeze the lemon half over the strawberries and add the sugar and salt. Gently mix, then set aside for at least 15 minutes.

7. **Make the whipped cream.** Using an electric mixer, beat the cream and sugar for about 2 minutes at medium to high speed until you have medium-soft peaks—do not overbeat.

8. **Assemble.** Slice each biscuit in half, top with some of the strawberries, then a dollop of whipped cream, then some more strawberries. Make sure you get some of the strawberry syrup from the bottom of the bowl!

GET CREATIVE: The most important trick to making a good biscuit is not overworking the dough when you are mixing and rolling it.

MEASUREMENT CONVERSIONS

	US STANDARD	US STANDARD (OUNCES)	METRIC (APPROXIMATE)
VOLUME EQUIVALENTS (LIQUID)	2 tablespoons	1 fl. oz.	30 mL
	¼ cup	2 fl. oz.	60 mL
	½ cup	4 fl. oz.	120 mL
	1 cup	8 fl. oz.	240 mL
	1½ cups	12 fl. oz.	355 mL
	2 cups or 1 pint	16 fl. oz.	475 mL
	4 cups or 1 quart	32 fl. oz.	1 L
	1 gallon	128 fl. oz.	4 L
VOLUME EQUIVALENTS (DRY)	⅛ teaspoon		0.5 mL
	¼ teaspoon		1 mL
	½ teaspoon		2 mL
	¾ teaspoon		4 mL
	1 teaspoon		5 mL
	1 tablespoon		15 mL
	¼ cup		59 mL
	⅓ cup		79 mL
	½ cup		118 mL
	⅝ cup		156 mL
	¾ cup		177 mL
	1 cup		235 mL
	2 cups or 1 pint		475 mL
	3 cups		700 mL
	4 cups or 1 quart		1 L
	½ gallon		2 L
	1 gallon		4 L
WEIGHT EQUIVALENTS	½ ounce		15 g
	1 ounce		30 g
	2 ounces		60 g
	4 ounces		115 g
	8 ounces		225 g
	12 ounces		340 g
	16 ounces or 1 pound		455 g

	FAHRENHEIT (F)	CELSIUS (C) (APPROXIMATE)
OVEN TEMPERATURES	250°F	120°F
	300°F	150°C
	325°F	180°C
	375°F	190°C
	400°F	200°C
	425°F	220°C
	450°F	230°C

INDEX

ACKNOWLEDGMENTS

To my sister, brother, and brother-in-law—who have always eaten my food, given me honest feedback, and been my biggest cheerleaders—I love you! To my amazing friends, who are more like family, you make life so much better—thank you! To the children in my life, who are always willing to help me on my many projects—Pia, Jack, Nino, Cooper, Piper, Laila, Imani, Bella, Tallie, Addy, and Walker—Auntie Jamaica loves you! To my nephews—KK, Noah, and Beau—I love our crazy modern family. To all my students, who have taught me to be a better teacher and to practice patience, thank you. To Team JAMaROO, who does amazing work every day, thank you for enriching the lives of so many children and helping me make my dreams come true. To my foodie friends, thank you for sharing cookbooks and recipes, exploring new restaurants, and taking cooking classes with me. To the Callisto Team, who gave me such an amazing opportunity with this book, thank you for your help along the way.

ABOUT THE AUTHOR

 **Jamaica Stevens**'s love for cooking started as a child, when she discovered Julia Child and Jacques Pépin on PBS. She continued to explore cooking by working for a catering company in college and eventually doing her own catering for small gatherings. Over the years, Jamaica has taken dozens of cooking classes, read countless cookbooks, and tested out recipes with her students during her time as a preschool teacher. Jamaica founded JAMaROO Kids in 2004 after teaching preschool for more than seven years. JAMaROO Kids specializes in providing enrichment programs, including dance, music, yoga, cooking, art, and bilingual classes. Currently, Jamaica leads a team of educators who specialize in teaching enrichment classes at more than 100 schools. She enjoys leading workshops, presenting at conferences all over the United States, and creating free content for the JAMaROO Kids YouTube Channel! When Jamaica does have downtime, you can find her in the kitchen creating recipes for her students, family, and friends.

Printed in the USA
CPSIA information can be obtained
at www.ICGtesting.com
CBHW041158090424
6568CB00007B/74

9 781648 769382